THE
MURDER
FILES

THE MURDER FILES

HISTORY'S GREATEST SECRETS REVEALED

SAM PILGER

NEW BURLINGTON

This edition first published in 2021 by
New Burlington Books,
The Old Brewery, 6 Blundell Street,
London N7 9BH, United Kingdom.

ISBN 978-1-80242-014-2

Conceived, designed, and produced by
The Bright Press, an imprint of the Quarto Group,
The Old Brewery, 6 Blundell Street,
London N7 9BH, United Kingdom.
T (0)20 7700 6700
www.QuartoKnows.com

PUBLISHER: James Evans
EDITORIAL DIRECTOR: Isheeta Mustafi
ART DIRECTOR: James Lawrence
MANAGING EDITOR: Jacqui Sayers
COMMISSIONING EDITOR: Abbie Sharman
PROJECT EDITOR: Katie Crous
DESIGN: Kevin Knight

Printed in Singapore

10 9 8 7 6 5 4 3 2 1

Cover picture: Shutterstock

CONTENTS

Introduction **6**

INTRODUCTION

There has long been a macabre fascination with the grisly world of murderers and serial killers. It appalls, scares, and unsettles us, but we cannot turn away from learning more about what motivates a person to take the life of another.

There is an uneasy shot of adrenaline on offer to those of us who delve into this dark world, driven by a need to come to understand the most destructive side of some of human nature. But there is also a protective sense that if we can arm ourselves with the facts of previous murders, it might possibly help to keep us safe.

In the *Murder Files* we take a look at some of history's most disturbing and horrific murders that have gripped and disgusted in equal measure, from every corner of the world, from the 19th century to the present day.

Serial killers cause particular fascination; the idea that an individual can get a thrill and a taste for murdering people over and over again. We investigate the mysterious Jack the Ripper, who murdered five women on the streets of East London during his reign of terror; as well as Belle Gunness, who is believed to have killed two husbands before becoming a serial killer at her Indiana farm. How did the seemingly respectable British doctor Harold Shipman evade justice for so long as he killed up to 250 patients? John Wayne Gacy became known as the "Killer Clown" as he entertained children by day, and at night lured up to 33 boys to his house before raping and murdering them.

Celebrity murders have always captivated the imagination; the thought that fame and fortune cannot protect you. How was the legendary fashion designer Gianni Versace murdered on his doorstep at home in Miami? What lay behind the death of the actress Sharon Tate, who was bludgeoned to death at her Los Angeles home?

Unsolved murders can fascinate us most, as they upset our natural desire to understand what happened, and to have real answers. What happened to the six-year-old beauty pageant queen JonBenét Ramsey, who was found dead in the basement of her family house in Colorado? And what could possibly explain the massacre of an entire family at the remote Hinterkaifeck Farm in Germany in 1922?

There are also **gruesome murders** that can be particularly difficult to comprehend, and simply defy belief that someone could inflict such suffering on others. The inspiration for Alfred Hitchcock's iconic movie *Psycho* was Ed Gein, who murdered two women and dug up bodies from graves in the middle of the night to use human skin for lamps, suits, seat covers, and gloves. In Hong Kong, a young woman was tortured over the course of a month before being murdered and dismembered. The three killers placed her skull inside a Hello Kitty plush toy doll.

While you will be shocked, saddened, and unsettled by these cases, they are sure to engross you by equal measure, in a bid to understand the events and theories behind the world's most fascinating *Murder Files*.

Was Robert F. Kennedy shot by a lone gunman, or does the evidence point toward at least one other?

1
SERIAL KILLERS

The bleak world of serial killers
has the power to both disturb
and fascinate, as we look
at nine cases of some of the
world's very worst, including
the Chessboard Killer Alexander
Pichushkin, who killed 48 in
Russia, The Beast of Colombia,
Luis Garavito, who killed 138,
and the Wests, who between
them claimed multiple victims
on an ordinary street in an
English town.

JACK
THE RIPPER

LOCATION:......WHITECHAPEL, LONDON, UK

VICTIMS: 5

DATE: 1888

Over the course of 10 weeks, a mysterious serial killer stalked the dark alleyways of Whitechapel in Victorian London.

During this short reign of terror, Jack the Ripper mutilated and killed at least five women but was able to avoid capture, and has never been identified.

Who was one of the world's most infamous serial killers?

THE EVENTS

The Ripper first struck in the early hours of August 31, 1888, when the body of Mary Ann Nichols, who had fled from her husband and five children, and was believed to be working as a prostitute, was found in Whitechapel. Her body had been mutilated with savage cuts to her throat and genital area, while her abdomen had been sliced open to reveal her bowel.

Only eight days later, the body of another prostitute, Annie Chapman, who had been complaining of feeling unwell and needed somewhere to spend the night, was found in nearby Spitalfields, with a deep cut to her throat and abdomen. But this time the killer had also cut out some of her stomach and intestines and placed them on her shoulders. Some of her uterus, bladder, and vagina had been completely removed.

A sketched scene from 1891 showing the discovery of one of Jack the Ripper's five victims.

On September 30, the Ripper claimed another life, when the body of Elizabeth Stride, who had spent the previous day earning money cleaning at a lodging house, was discovered in Whitechapel. She had also had her throat cut, but did not share the same abdominal injuries as the first two victims. It has been speculated her body was less mutilated as the killer had been interrupted, and a man called Israel Schwartz believed he had seen her being attacked 15 minutes before she was found, but thought it a domestic dispute.

Just 45 minutes later, another horrifically mutilated body was found in nearby Mitre Square. This was Catherine Eddowes, whose last words to her partner John Kelly, who had been worried about the presence of this serial killer, were: "Don't you fear for me, I'll take care of myself, and I shall not fall into his hands." It was a promise she could not keep, and instead she had her

The mutilated body of Catherine Eddowes was found here, in Mitre Square.

throat cut and was disemboweled. The killer had removed her uterus and left kidney. She had also had her face disfigured with large Vs cut into her cheeks and eyelids.

On the morning of November 9, landlord John McCarthy went to ask his tenant Mary Kelly for the late rent for her room at Miller's Court in Spitalfields—only to find she had become the Ripper's fifth, and probably final, victim. "On the bed was all that remained of the young woman," McCarthy recalled. "There was little left of her, not much more than a skeleton. Her face was terribly scarred and mutilated. All this was horrifying enough, but the mental picture of that sight which remains most vividly with me is the poor woman's eyes. They were wide open, and seemed to be staring straight at me with a look of terror."

THE THEORIES

After each of the five murders the Ripper was able to slip away into the night without being captured, and left very few incriminating clues behind. Over the course of their investigation the police interviewed 2,000 people and detained 80, with special attention paid to butchers and surgeons, but they never came close to finding the Ripper's true identity.

In the 130 years since the murders, more than 500 suspects have been named, but none have ever come close to sticking. The name "Jack" derives from a letter that was passed to the police in September 1888, but it could have been a hoax, and it has never been confirmed it was sent by the killer.

An array of suspects

As recently as 2014, armchair detective Russell Edwards claimed the Ripper was 23-year-old Polish barber Aaron Kosminski, who lived in the East End at the time of the murders. In 2007 Russell had bought a blood-stained shawl, which had been found by the body of Catherine Eddowes, and tested it for DNA, which he claims matched that of Kosminski. However, others have dismissed the shawl as having been contaminated for over a century and consequently unreliable.

The most sensational theory is that the Ripper was Queen Victoria's grandson Prince Albert Victor, who was known to family as Eddy. It was said he had contracted syphilis from his visits to East End brothels, causing him

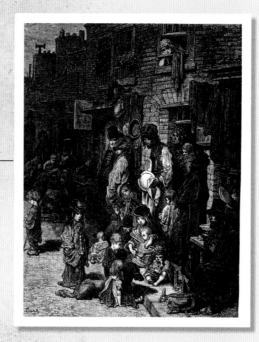

The squalid
streets of
Whitechapel
provided
the perfect
hunting
ground for
the Ripper.

BACKGROUND

Toward the end of the 19th century, Whitechapel in the East End of London
had become a seething melting pot of crime, poverty, and dilapidated housing.
This overcrowded and filthy area was also home to as many as 62 brothels and
1,200 prostitutes, as desperate women did what they could to survive.

It was against this backdrop in 1888 that a mysterious serial killer, who would
become known around the world as "Jack the Ripper," stalked the dark street
corners to murder five women in just a 10-week spell. There are some who
have sought to attribute six more murders to the killer, as they occurred in
Whitechapel between April 1888 and February 1891, but at the time the local
police believed only those known as "the canonical five" were definitely the
work of the Ripper.

to go insane and embark on the five murders. Yet there is no evidence to support this, and he was believed to have been out of London at the time of the murders.

German-born artist Walter Sickert became another suspect after he produced a series of paintings of naked prostitutes that some suggested were very similar to the autopsy pictures of the Ripper's victims. One of his paintings was even entitled *Jack the Ripper's Bedroom*. In 2002 American crime writer Patricia Cornwell published her book *Portrait of a Killer: Jack the Ripper—Case Closed*, in which she argued that a team of experts had found Sickert's DNA on the "Jack" letters. There was, however, no evidence Sickert was even in London in late 1888, and some have placed him in France.

The London detective Sir Melville McNaughton has suggested Montague John Druitt was the Ripper, as the murders stopped following his suicide. A barrister and former schoolteacher, Druitt was believed to have been seen in Whitechapel at the time of the murders, and his body was found floating in the Thames river a month after the Ripper's final victim, Mary Kelly, was killed. A search of Druitt's house would find a note from him saying he deserved to die, as he believed he was going insane, but nothing connecting him to the murders.

THE
BLACK

WIDOW

LOCATION:..... LA PORTE, INDIANA, USA

SUSPECT: ....BELLE GUNNESS

VICTIMS: 14

DATE: 1884-1908

When Asle Helgelien went searching for his missing brother Andrew, he found him buried in a hog pen next to 13 other victims.

Belle Gunness had killed them all for profit, but after apparently staging her own death in a fire, was never seen again.

What happened to the original Black Widow?

THE EVENTS

In 1881 Brynhild Paulsdatter Storset left behind her life of grinding poverty as a dairy maid on a farm in Norway for a new start in the United States. Joining her older sister Nellie in Chicago, she changed her name to something more American: Bella Petersen.

Three years later, Petersen would marry her first husband Mads Sorensen, and the couple opened a candy store in Chicago. The store was not a great success, and within a year had mysteriously burned to the ground. The couple received a large payout from their insurance policy, which they used to buy a family home for their three daughters, Myrtle, Lucy, and Jennie.

On July 30, 1890, Mads Sorensen died in mysterious circumstances. The first doctor to examine him believed he had been poisoned with strychnine, with Bella admitting she had given him some form of "medicinal powders," but the family doctor dismissed it as heart failure.

On the day of his death, Sorensen had two overlapping life insurance policies, which provided his widow Bella with a handsome payout of $5,000, which she used to buy a 42-acre farm in La Porte, Indiana.

She would change her name again to Belle, and in 1901 married the town's butcher, widower Peter Gunness. Within a year, Peter's daughter died in Bella's care, and he himself would die in strange

Belle Gunness with three of her children (from left to right): Lucy, Myrtle, and Phillip.

circumstances when it was reported a sausage grinder and a jar of scalding water fell on his head. A coroner reported his belief Peter had been poisoned, as he showed symptoms of having ingested strychnine, but it was ruled an accidental death—and Bella walked away with another insurance payout.

While Belle would not marry again, in January 1908 Andrew Helgelien from South Dakota accepted her invitation to join her in Indiana. She had told him, "Come prepared to stay forever." Helgelien promptly emptied his bank account and moved in with her, but was never seen again.

Unearthing the bodies

On the morning of April 28, 1908, a fire broke out at the farmhouse, and in the burning ruins a body of a headless woman was found, believed to be Belle, lying alongside her three children.

Asle Helgelien, who had been in correspondence with Belle about his missing brother, insisted that the authorities now take a closer look at her property. They found some disturbed areas of dirt in the farm's hog pens, and after digging down 3 feet (1 meter) discovered a foul-smelling gunny sack filled with human remains, including two hands, two feet, and a head. When the dismembered body parts were all laid out, it became obvious they belonged to Andrew Helgelien.

A total of 14 bodies were found, including men, women, children, and an infant. One was Belle's foster daughter Jennie Olsen, who was believed to have been studying in California; however, the vast majority of the butchered bodies could not be identified. The apparently kindly mother had been revealed to be a serial killer.

THE THEORIES

The one constant in Belle's life had been her farmhand Ray Lamphere, but in the years before the fire their relationship had become strained, and she had reported him to the police as a danger to her family. Lamphere was arrested soon after the fire, and in November 1908 convicted of arson, but not murder, and sentenced to a minimum of two years in prison. Just 15 months later, Lamphere would die in prison, but not before he was believed to have made a confession on his deathbed to a local priest.

Lamphere detailed how Belle had lured a succession of men to her property with a classified ad she placed in the "matrimonial columns" of local Norwegian-language newspapers: "WANTED: A woman who owns a beautifully located and valuable farm in first-class condition, wants a good and reliable man as partner in the same. Some little cash is required for which will be furnished first-class security." When the men arrived, they were robbed and killed by Belle, with Lamphere's assistance. She would slip drugs into their coffee before delivering a fatal blow to the head with a meat cleaver. Their bodies would be cut up in her basement and buried outside around her hog pen.

With Asle Helgelien close to discovering her secret, it was believed Belle decided to burn her house down, stage a getaway, and start again somewhere new. Lamphere claimed Belle had traveled to Chicago a couple of days before the fire to find her body double. They had recruited a woman who thought she would be the farm's maid, but who had been beheaded, dressed in Belle's clothes, and left to burn in the fire.

The body found in the ruins was 5 feet 4 inches (1.6 meters) and weighed around 73 pounds (33 kg), whereas Belle was a far bigger and stockier woman, standing 5 feet 10 inches (1.8 meters) tall and weighing more than 200 pounds (90 kg). However, the coroner at the inquest into the fire ruled the headless body was Belle after they found a piece of bridgework featuring two human teeth, porcelain teeth, and a gold crown her dentist confirmed he had made for her.

Rumors have long persisted that Belle did not die in the fire, and in the years that followed there were sightings of her around the United States. The most credible was of a woman called Esther Carlson, who in 1931 was arrested for poisoning a Norwegian-American man in Los Angeles. She looked like Belle, and was the same size, but died while awaiting trial, and modern DNA comparisons proved inconclusive.

THE
SORCERER

LOCATION:...NORTH SUMATRA, INDONESIA

SUSPECT:.................AHMAD SURADJI

VICTIMS:..............................42

DATE:...........................1986-97

When a farmer discovered a strange mound of dirt in a sugarcane field, it would soon lead him to unearth the recently killed body of a 21-year-old girl.

Alongside her in the field, Asia's fifth-most prolific serial killer, Ahmad Suradji, had buried 41 other victims, after routinely sucking out their saliva.

What motivated the Sorcerer to claim so many young lives?

THE EVENTS

In many parts of Indonesia, especially in the remote rural areas, there has long been a strong veneration of sorcery and supernatural powers. A *dukun*, the Indonesian term for a shaman, is seen to be invested with these special powers and is a healer, spirit medium, and purveyor of black magic.

In the village of Aman Damai in the Indonesian province of North Sumatra, Ahmad Suradji set up himself up as the local dukun, and invited people from far and wide to visit him, to benefit from his powers. He had previously served time in prison for a variety of petty crimes, including cattle theft. He wanted to leave that life behind and follow a righteous path, so decided to become a sorcerer like his father before him. "I aspired to follow in the footsteps of my father," he would say during his subsequent trial. "I did not learn sorcery from anyone else but my father."

He became a revered member of the community, and was also known as Datuk Maringgi, with locals believing he could heal the sick, help them enjoy better lives, and even part the clouds above them. This reputation would become a front for Suradji to feed his desire to kill, as he found it an effective way to lure women to his house.

Ritualistic killing

As part of his killing ritual, Suradji would ask the women to dig their own graves and stand waist-deep inside, which they thought was part of their cure and would help them benefit from his powers. But Suradji would instead use the fact that they were now immobilized to strangle and kill them.

Suradji continued undisturbed for 11 years, during which time he murdered 42 women and left many of them in a sugarcane plantation field, with them purposefully staring at his nearby house to give him further power.

It was not until April 27, 1997, that a farmer accompanied by his livestock stumbled across a strange-looking mound of dirt in these fields. When he returned with five other men and started to dig beneath the mound, they were soon hit by a rancid smell, and discovered the naked body of a young girl. It was identified as 21-year-old Sri Kemala Dewi by her grieving mother. "It was like my worst nightmare had come to life. I refused to believe it was her, but there she was, dead in front of me," she said.

Ahmad Suradji lured his victims to sugarcane fields near his house before murdering them and sucking saliva from their mouths.

Three days earlier Dewi had left the family home to run an errand and not been seen again. A 15-year-old local rickshaw driver Andreas Suwito came forward to say he had dropped Dewi at Suradji's house. "She said she wanted to go to Datuk's house. I was curious because it was rather late at night, so I asked why she was going there and she had told me not to be too nosy," he said.

On a search of Suradji's house, the police found Dewi's bracelet and dress, and he admitted she had come to him for guidance, as she did not want her fiancé to leave her for another woman, and thought his powers could help her.

After four days of interrogation, Suradji confessed to the murders of 42 girls and women, and said he had buried them in the same sugarcane field. A massive excavation would find a collection of skulls, bones, and bodies there. Suradji would later be convicted of these murders, and after 11 years in prison, he was executed by a firing squad in July 2008.

THE THEORIES

In 1986 Suradji said he had had a dream in which his deceased sorcerer father had come to him and said he needed "the saliva of 70 dead young women in order to attain invincibility." But Suradji added that it was not his father's intention that he kill the women. "My father did not specifically advise me to kill people. So I was thinking, it would take ages if I have to wait to get 70 women. I was trying to get to it as fast as possible, I took my own initiative to kill."

In his role as a dukun he never aroused suspicion and had the benefit of the women voluntarily coming to his house. It was also a method to make money, for he still took his fees, estimated to be between $200 and $400, from the women before he killed them. "If I just robbed people, I could get shot or put in jail, but this way, people came to me. I took their money, then I killed them," he said. When the women had been killed and were stuck in the ground, he would lower himself down and suck saliva from their mouths.

There appears to have been no sexual motive to Suradji's serial killing. "He simply said it was also a way for him to make money as he could rob them without getting caught," said Alfred Satyo, the forensic expert assigned to the case.

Before he faced the firing squad, Suradji showed some regret: "The black magic came from God. I don't have it anymore, I have repented. I hope I have a chance to live," he said.

DOCTOR SHIPMAN'S MURDERS

LOCATION: ....NORTHERN ENGLAND, UK

SUSPECT: ....DR. HAROLD SHIPMAN

VICTIMS: ....250 (ESTIMATED)

DATE: 1975-99

"I don't believe in keeping them going," is how Dr. Shipman characterized his treatment of elderly patients a year before he was arrested.

Over the course of 24 years, Shipman murdered an estimated 250 people with a lethal injection of morphine, making him the most prolific serial killer in modern history.

What motivated the doctor, and how did he get away with it for so long?

THE EVENTS

In February 1976 Dr. Harold Shipman, a family doctor in the West Yorkshire town of Todmorden, was convicted of obtaining the drug meperidine, a form of morphine, by deception, to feed his own addiction. After receiving treatment, Shipman avoided being struck off and was allowed to continue practicing as a family doctor., first at the Donneybrook practice in Hyde, Greater Manchester, before he opened his own practice on the town's Market Street.

There he developed a reputation as an attentive and caring doctor. "Many patients describe Shipman as having a wonderful bedside manner, especially with the elderly," wrote Dame Janet Smith, who led the inquiry into his murders. "He would make much of them and sometimes tease them gently. They liked it. He made them feel that he was a real friend as well as their doctor. Yet he would kill them."

In March 1998 the alarm was first raised about Shipman by a mortician in Hyde, and a neighboring doctor's office, which noticed the death rate of Shipman's patients was double its own. The local coroner conveyed their concerns to Greater Manchester Police, who conducted a quick investigation that failed to contact Shipman or the relatives of any of his victims, and ultimately cleared him to kill again.

For nearly a quarter of a century, Harold Shipman took advantage of his position as a doctor to kill 250 of his patients.

The doctor was eventually stopped in June 1998, when Angela Woodruff, the daughter of his final victim, Kathleen Grundy, discovered her mother had surprisingly excluded her from her will but left Shipman £386,000 ($545,000). The police exhumed Grundy's body and found she contained traces of diacetylmorphine in her muscle tissues, which Shipman claimed was because she was a drug addict, but it was found he had added this comment after her death to cover his tracks. It was also established he had forged Grundy's will.

In September 1998 Shipman was arrested on suspicion of Grundy's murder. The police exhumed more bodies, and investigated 14 elderly women whose deaths Shipman had certified. They all followed the same pattern: he had injected them with a lethal dose of diacetylmorphine, signed their death certificates, and on his computer at his office, altered their medical records to falsely declare they had been unwell. He would kill patients who were on the brink of death with terminal illnesses, others who had poor-quality lives but were not dying, and some who were perfectly healthy with years to live.

In October 1999 Shipman stood trial at Preston Crown Court for the murders of 15 women he had killed with injections of diacetylmorphine between 1995 and 1998. Shipman always protested his innocence, but the jury refused to believe him, and in January 2000 found him guilty on all 15 counts of murder before the judge sentenced him to life in prison.

The police believed Shipman was responsible for a total of 171 deaths, the youngest aged 41 and the oldest 93, while The Shipman Inquiry settled on a figure between 215 and 250.

In January 2004, four years after his conviction, Shipman committed suicide at H.M. Prison Wakefield the day before his 58th birthday by hanging himself with his bedsheets from the bars on his window.

THE THEORIES

After two years of investigations that produced a 336-page, six-volume report, The Shipman Inquiry was unable to establish a firm motive for the estimated 250 murders.

"I regret to say that I can shed very little light on why Shipman killed his patients," Dame Janet Smith has admitted. "There is some evidence that he is an addictive personality, and it is possible that killing was a form of addiction...It is typical of addictive behavior that the subject needs more and more opportunities to feed the addiction."

Smith concluded Shipman took pleasure in being invested with power, and deciding who lived and who died. "He would be the center of attention and would take control. He would present himself as omniscient. He would give instructions about the removal of the body. He would give his explanation for the death, often saying that, although it might have been a surprise to the relatives, it had been no surprise to him."

In one instance, the inquiry found in February 1998 Stephen Dickson asked Shipman how long his father-in-law, cancer patient Harold Eddleston, had to live. "I wouldn't buy him any Easter eggs," Shipman replied, killing Eddleston four days later.

Some psychiatrists who examined Shipman before his trial came to believe his murders were proof of "classic necrophilia," which involves taking pleasure from being in the presence of death.

In the search for answers, because Shipman never spoke publicly about why he killed, some have looked back to his childhood and the death of his mother from cancer at the age of only 43. He was greatly impacted by her death while still a teenager, which inspired speculation he became angry later in his life at being surrounded by so many old people who had enjoyed far longer lives than his mother.

THE
BEAST OF
COLOMBIA

LOCATION: ....COLOMBIA

SUSPECT: ....LUIS GARAVITO

VICTIMS: ....138+

DATE: 1992-99

When Colombian police discovered the remains of 25 young boys buried in a ravine, they knew they had a mad man stalking the country.

Luis Garavito was able to elude them for seven years to become the world's second-most prolific serial killer—with a gruesome body count of 138.

How did "The Beast" get away with so many murders?

THE EVENTS

At the start of the 1990s, Colombia had been torn apart by a conflict that had lasted nearly three decades, as the government, far-right paramilitary organizations, left-wing guerilla groups, and the powerful drug cartels fought for control. It severely destabilized the entire country, dividing society, plunging people into poverty, and throwing them out of their homes and onto the streets, which in turn produced countless vulnerable children.

"Kids disappear all the time in Colombia, especially those from the poorer [communities]," Timothy W. Ross, who worked for Fundación Renacer, a charity helping young people, told *The New York Times* in 1999. "They tend to come from unstable homes anyway, but the deep social instability produced by military, political, and economic displacement has fragmented families further."

This would all prove to be fertile ground for a serial killer who preyed on children, and fueled a seven-year reign of terror in Colombia. Between 1992 and 1999, Garavito murdered a confirmed 138 young boys. However, the authorities believe the real total of victims could be as high as 300.

Disturbed and damaged

Garavito was born in 1957 in the town of Genova, in western Colombia. He experienced a traumatic childhood: his mother worked as a prostitute; his father would beat him regularly. There are reports his alcoholic father would also force his children, including Luis, to watch his mother having sex with her clients, and aged only eight he was the victim of a sustained sexual assault by a local pedophile.

After spending up to five years in psychiatric care, Garavito was unable to hold down a regular job and would drink heavily. Aged around 35, he began to develop an urge to abuse and kill children.

His victims were almost always young boys, aged between six and 16, who were desperate, orphaned, and living on the streets. Garavito would dress in a variety of disguises—including as a monk, a priest, a farmer, a kindly older man, or a shop owner—before approaching them and pretending to be their savior by offering them a job, a place to stay, or a meal.

Luis Garavito adopted several different appearances to win the trust of his young victims.

The children would eagerly accept and follow Garavito to a secluded area, often on the edge of towns, before he would discard his disguise and reveal his true intentions. The boys would be stripped and have their hands bound, before being subjected to sexual abuse, rape, and torture. Many of his victims had their throats slit, were bitten all over their bodies, and anally violated. Several even had their testicles cut off and stuffed in their mouths.

Few noticed as dozens of children went missing—then 25 skeletons of young boys were discovered in a ravine in the city of Pereira. The police thought they had uncovered evidence of a satanic ritual, until they realized this was the work of a serial killer, and a national taskforce was formed to find him.

Over the course of two days in February 1998, the bodies of three young boys were found outside of Genova. They bore the signature marks of Garavito's victims: bound hands, slit throats, and evidence of sexual abuse.

A note at the scene led police to a house owned by Garavito's friend, where they found he had left a bag containing photos of young boys and a journal containing details of the murders. On April 22, 1999, the 42-year-old Garavito was arrested by local police in Villavicencio for the attempted kidnap of a 12-year-old boy, after a homeless man had thwarted him.

THE THEORIES

Garavito would quickly confess to the murders of up to 138 young boys in 60 towns across Colombia, and also across the border in Ecuador. "Yes, I killed them, and I ask for forgiveness for all that I have done," he told police.

"We are not facing some sort of criminal genius," said Pablo Elias Gonzalez, the director of the state prosecutor's investigative team. "We are confronting an individual who had no inhibiting restraints to killing."

Garavito was able to take advantage of Colombia's internal strife to get away with his killings for seven long years. "These were poor kids that nobody cares about, and that is why this went on for so long before they did anything about it," Norma Garzon Duque, a Colombian street vendor told *The New York Times* in 1999. "If it had been rich kids disappearing like that, the cops would have been on top of the case from the beginning."

The serial killer was charged with 172 counts of murder, and found guilty of 138 of them, for which he was given a sentence of 1,853 years and 9 days, the longest in Colombian history; but it was for show, and was soon reduced to as low as 22 years because he helped the police to locate many of the bodies. Garavito is currently serving his sentence at a maximum-security prison in Valledupar and could be due for release as soon as 2023. He has talked about wanting to become a politician and draft legislation to help defend children.

THE
KILLER

CLOWN

LOCATION: .... CHICAGO, ILLINOIS, USA

SUSPECT: .... JOHN WAYNE GACY

VICTIMS: .... 33+

DATE: 1972-78

In December 1978, underneath an ordinary ranch house in the
Chicago suburbs, police discovered the bones and remains of
26 young men.

Within days, John Wayne Gacy would confess to having murdered
a total of 33 men over the course of just six years.

How did the Killer Clown lure so many young men to their deaths?

THE EVENTS

At the start of the 1970s, John Wayne Gacy was living in the Chicago suburbs as a respected owner of the construction company PDM Contractors. He was considered a kind man by his neighbors, and would host summer parties for them at his house in Norridge, in the Norwood Park township. He was also active in his local Democratic party, and would even meet President Carter's wife, the First Lady Rosalynn Carter, in May 1978.

By 1975 Gacy had also started performing as a clown in his spare time at children's hospitals, charity events, and local parties. He would dress up in colorful suits and full makeup as clowns he called Pogo or Patches. He would later say he loved entertaining children as a clown, allowing him to enjoy "relaxation" time, and evoke happy memories of his own childhood. It also helped him foster a misleading image as a warm and fun character.

In his spare time John Wayne Gacy entertained children as a clown at parties, charity events, and local hospitals.

AS POGO THE CLOWN

Unbeknown to the parents and children at these parties, Gacy had been convicted of sodomizing 15-year-old Donald Voorhees in Waterloo, Iowa, in August 1967. Though he was sentenced to 10 years in prison in November 1968, he only served 18 months, and was released in June 1970.

Despite still being on parole, Gacy continued to prey on young men, and in February 1971 was charged with sexually assaulting a teenage boy in Chicago, but the case collapsed when the victim refused to appear. Four months later he was charged with aggravated sexual battery when another boy accused him of forcing him to perform oral sex on him, but again it never went to court.

On January 3, 1972, Gacy went a step further and committed his first murder after he had picked up 16-year-old Timothy McCoy from the Greyhound bus station in Chicago, with the promise of a sightseeing tour of the city and a warm bed for the night before he continued his journey to Nebraska. Instead, Gacy would attack McCoy with a knife inside his house the following morning, stabbing him multiple times in the chest. He would then bury the body in what was known as a crawl space underneath his house. Over the next seven years, Gacy would kill another 32 men, and store the vast majority of their bodies in this same crawl space.

Luring multiple victims

Gacy would usually lure his victims to his house to have a drink or take drugs, to have sex if they were a male prostitute, or to discuss a job at his construction company. He found the victims late at night on the streets; some were forced into his car, while others were fooled by Gacy pretending to be a police officer. After tricking his victims into wearing a pair of handcuffs, they were then powerless to stop him raping and torturing them. He would often hold their heads under water in his bath before finally killing them by placing a rope tourniquet around their necks and slowly strangling them.

Within 24 hours he would bury the bodies in the crawl space underneath his house. Two boys, David Cram and Michael Rossi, who worked with Gacy and lived at the house for short periods, had dug trenches in the space, which they were told was for a plumbing project. Gacy had added lime on the ground to cover up the rotting smell of the bodies. "It was right in front of the closet, that opens into the trap into the basement," Gacy would later tell his defense lawyers. "I opened up the trap, and I just threw him down there."

```
Name:
John Wayne Gacy
D.O.B.: March 17, 1942
Description: Male,
5 ft 9 in. (175 cm)
graying hair,
dark eyes
Charge: Murder,
33 counts
```

BACKGROUND

Born in Chicago in 1942, Gacy was regularly assaulted by his alcoholic father, sometimes with a leather belt. He would have a closer relationship with his mother and two sisters, but this enraged his father further, who would call him a "Mama's boy" and suggested he was a homosexual.

In 1950, at the age of eight, Gacy had recalled how he was sexually assaulted by a contractor who had been working on an empty lot next to his family's house in Chicago. He went on a trip with the man on the promise of getting some ice cream, but instead was abused by him inside his car.

As a teenager Gacy spent nearly a year in hospital after suffering a series of fainting spells and blackouts. He also had a heart condition that stopped him playing sports. When he was 18, Gacy ran away to Las Vegas for a few months and took a job at a mortuary. He lived next to an embalming room, and took part in 86 funerals. One night he climbed into a coffin containing the body of a young boy, and found himself with an erection. This episode unsettled him, and he returned to Chicago not long afterward.

He married his first wife Marlynn in 1964, and the couple had a son and a daughter, but she divorced him after his conviction for sodomy in 1968. In 1972 he married Carole Hoff, who already had two daughters, but they divorced after only three years.

Police found several bodies underneath Gacy's house in the Chicago suburb of Norridge.

Gacy had attempted to implicate Cram and Rossi in the murders, but Michael Albrecht, a policeman who helped catch him, has stated that he acted alone, and there has never been any evidence he had any help.

By 1978 the crawl space had become full of bodies, forcing Gacy to now dispose of them in the Des Plaines River, or bury them in his garden.

In December of that year, 15-year-old Robert Piest went missing from a pharmacy in Des Plaines after he had told his mother he was going to have a brief conversation with Gacy about working for his company. Within an hour, Gacy had raped and killed Piest at his house before throwing his body in the Des Plaines River. But Gacy had become sloppy, and when police obtained a search warrant to his house the next morning, they found a receipt from a colleague of Piest's from the pharmacy. The next day, police would also find a high-school ring belonging to John Szyc, an earlier victim.

Gacy was put under police surveillance, and when he was seen with marijuana, they were able to arrest him, on December 21, and conduct another search of his house, which is when they discovered the door to the crawl space. Here in the dark they quickly found a collection of bones and remains belonging to the victims.

The very next day, Gacy confessed to killing a total of 33 young men, and drew detailed maps where the police could find their remains. Over the course of the following week, the police would unearth the bodies of 26 young men in the crawl space, and three elsewhere on his property.

Initially charged with the murders of seven men in January 1979, by April that year Gacy was indicted for another 26. His trial began in February 1980, and his lawyers argued unsuccessfully he was not guilty due to insanity. The jury voted unanimously to convict him of all 33 murders, and he was sentenced to death. On May 10, 1994, after a last meal of Kentucky Fried Chicken, Gacy was killed by lethal injection at the Stateville Correctional Center in Crest Hill, Illinois.

THE THEORIES

After his conviction, Gacy admitted he had been sexually aroused when he committed murder. When he stabbed his first victim, Timothy McCoy, the sound of his last breaths, what he called "gurgulations," gave him an intense orgasm. "That's when I realized that death was the ultimate thrill," he said.

"He was absolutely a sociopath," one of his lawyers, Bob Motta, told NBC Chicago in 2021. "And his inability to have any kind of empathy was chilling." Motta confirmed that Gacy never showed any remorse for killing so many young men. He convinced himself they had known what they were participating in.

"There's not one of them that didn't die through their own hand or their own wrongdoing," he told Motta in a taped conversation. "If you want to say I tempted them, put them into temptation, yes...Everybody came to my house willingly, understandably, and knowing what's going to happen."

THE
CHESSBOARD
KILLER

LOCATION: ....MOSCOW, RUSSIA

SUSPECT: ....ALEXANDER PICHUSHKIN

VICTIMS: ....48+

DATE: 1992-2006

It was only after the police began to notice bodies appearing in the city's sewage system that they realized a prolific serial killer was on the loose.

For five years Alexander Pichushkin enjoyed luring his victims into woods before murdering them and pushing them into deep wells.

What motivated "The Chessboard Killer" to claim up to 48 victims?

THE EVENTS

Pichushkin claimed his first victim when he was 18, in July 1992. He had gone for a walk with an old school friend Mikhail Odichuk and told him about his interest in killing. He suggested they find a victim and do it together. Odichuk thought his friend was probably joking, but Pichushkin became annoyed when he realized his friend didn't share his desires, and killed him instead. The police questioned him, but no charges were brought.

He would wait another nine years before he could summon up the courage to murder again. In May 2001 he killed Yevgeny Pronin, then embarked on an eight-week spree that saw him claim another nine victims. Pichushkin would briefly pause before killing another five people later that year, during the fall and winter. He chose victims that no one would miss—pensioners with no relatives, the homeless, drunks, and drug addicts. Pichushkin looked for victims in his own neighborhood on the southwest outskirts of Moscow, especially at the 2,700-acre Bitsa Park that was just a five-minute walk from his apartment.

He would wait, sometimes for hours, until they were on their own, and possibly drunk. They were normally men. He would saunter over and suggest they went on a walk through the woods. He would then produce a bottle of vodka and get them even drunker, before suggesting a toast to his imaginary dead dog. He would strike his victims over the head with a hammer, before sometimes forcing pieces of his broken vodka bottle into their head wounds. He would often take his victims to near the edge of the wells in the woods, then push their bludgeoned bodies inside to fall down 30 feet (9 meters).

Pichushkin offered his victims a drink of vodka before smashing the bottle over their head.

Name: Alexander
Pichushkin
D.O.B.: April 9, 1974
Description: Male,
graying hair,
dark eyes
Charge: Multiple
murders

BACKGROUND

No one had ever paid Alexander Pichushkin much attention; the 32-year-old supermarket worker from the outskirts of the Russian capital Moscow had always seemed an unremarkable but perfectly decent man. His own mother Natasha called him "ordinary," and his manager at work said he was "good natured" and "polite and well mannered" with customers.

Pichushkin still lived at home with his mother Natasha and his younger sister Katya, but behind this normal exterior, he harbored a desire to become known as one of the world's most prolific serial killers. As a child, he had enjoyed playing chess with his grandfather, but by the time he was a teenager, Pichushkin had declared his wish was to place a coin on each of a chessboard's 64 squares to represent each of his murder victims.

After he had been convicted of his crimes, a childhood accident at a playground suddenly became more relevant. When he was young, Pichushkin had been struck in the head by a swing, which might have caused significant damage to the frontal cortex of his brain, and, in time, made him become more aggressive. In the wake of the accident, Pichushkin's mother noticed his personality change and he became more insular and agitated; Pichushkin was moved to a new school for children with learning disabilities.

Out of the shadows

In November 2005 Pichushkin claimed his 41st victim when he killed 63-year-old former policeman Nikolai Zakharchenko. Finally, here was a victim the police would take notice of, and they duly launched an investigation. Pichushkin had been murdering in the shadows, but now the authorities realized they had a serial killer in their midst. "The Bitsa Park Killer" was now all over the news; children were kept at home, and the park would often be empty.

In July 2006 Pichushkin became uncharacteristically sloppy, as if he wanted to be caught, when he murdered what would prove to be his final victim. He went for a walk with Marina Moskalyova, who worked with him at the supermarket. She had left her son a note to say she had gone out with Pichushkin, and there would later be footage of the pair boarding the Moscow metro. When her body was found in the park, he was the obvious suspect, and it linked him to all the ones that had gone before.

The sprawling Bitsa Park, on the southwest outskirts of Moscow, is where Pichushkin found many of his victims.

Pichushkin once declared
he wanted to kill 64 people,
to represent every square
on a chessboard.

On July 16, 2006, at around midnight, Pichushkin's mother opened the door to a group of heavily armed riot police who had come to apprehend her son. He did not resist, and very quickly admitted to all his murders, claiming his final count was as high as 63. A year later, in October 2007, following an exhaustive trial, Pichushkin was convicted of murdering 48 people. He was sentenced to life imprisonment, and will never be set free.

THE THEORIES

Pichushkin killed to be famous: each of the 48 lives he claimed was his way of becoming somebody, and for the world to know who he was. Before he was arrested, he had been watching television with his mother and sister when a news report mentioned "The Bitsa Park Killer." His sister wondered who it could be, and he had been desperate to admit it was him.

When he was finally arrested, he wasn't shy or evasive about his crimes; he wanted to tell the police everything. "We were in shock when we realized how many people he'd killed," the chief investigator Andrei Suprunenko told *GQ* in 2009. "In the beginning, we only had 13 bodies. And then Pichushkin began to tell us that he'd killed more than 60 people…All maniacs want to talk. It made him feel important. I told him I admired him, and he liked that, and then he opened up. It was very important for Pichushkin that people think he was a hero, so I made him feel like a hero."

No regrets

His defense lawyer Pavel Ivannikov said, with a note of surprise, that his client "confessed to everything he was accused of and some things he was not. He regrets nothing, which for me is strange."

The killer's plan to fill each square of a chessboard gave him even greater fame, but the authorities believe he would never have stopped at just 64.

"There was total shock when we heard it was Pichushkin," Natasha Fyedosova has said about the man who killed her father Boris as his 36th victim. "He was always very calm, always by himself. I thought it was strange that he only wanted to kill people he knew. If he had killed people he didn't know, in another neighborhood, it wouldn't have been as bad, but he killed people he knew."

Pichushkin spoke about his murders with a misplaced sense of romance: "A first killing is like your first love. You never forget it," he said during his trial. Prosecutors said tests on him had shown he apparently didn't have any mental health problems, although he was found to have signs of "homocidomania," which is a fascination with killing.

THE
BRAZILIAN
MANIAC

LOCATION: ....BRAZIL

SUSPECT: ....PEDRO RODRIGUES FILHO

VICTIMS: ....70-100 (ESTIMATED)

DATE: 1967-2003

The sixth most prolific serial killer in history, Pedro Rodrigues Filho is believed to have killed between 70 and 100 men.

He murdered his first victim at 14, by 18 he had killed 10, and he would continue to murder even when placed behind bars.

What motivated the Brazilian to kill so many?

THE EVENTS

Pedro Rodrigues Filho had a traumatic start to life, being born in 1954 with a bruised and deformed skull after his father had kicked his mother in the stomach while she was pregnant. Growing up in Santa Rita do Sapucai, in the southeastern Brazilian state of Minas Gerais, the young Rodrigues was surrounded by death at a young age, working in a poultry slaughterhouse.

He also spoke about having an urge to kill. It is reported he nearly acted on this when he was 13 years old, in a fight with an older cousin, but he resisted and let his cousin survive. A year later, Filho killed for the first time when he shot the deputy mayor of his hometown with his grandfather's shotgun. He was exacting revenge after the mayor had said his father had stolen food from a school. He would later explain, "His mistake was to have accused my father of theft."

Pedro Rodrigues Filho grew up in Santa Rita do Sapucai, in the southeastern Brazilian state of Minas Gerais.

It was reported Filho fled to Mogi das Cruzes, in Greater Sao Paulo, where he proceeded to kill several drug dealers who infested the city. He began a romance with Maria Aparecida Olympia; some reports say they married, but she was murdered by a drug gang when seven months pregnant with their child. Filho went looking for her murderers, and was tipped off that some were attending a wedding. He and four friends arrived unannounced and killed seven guests. It was estimated that after this, by the age of 18, Rodrigues had already killed 10 people.

According to an interview with *Noticias* in Brazil, he killed his father, Pedro Rodrigues, as revenge for killing his mother, Manuela, with 21 machete blows. He stabbed his father purposefully once more, with a total of 22 wounds, before allegedly tearing out his heart, chewing it, and spitting it out.

Prison killings
In May 1973 Rodrigues, who had earned the nickname Pedrinho Matador (Killer Petey), was jailed for at least 11 murders, but this did not stop him increasing his body count. Over the next 34 years, it is estimated he killed up to 47 more men while in prison. He killed rapists and cellmates he didn't like, and once, according to Terra.com.br, killed a man by beheading him with a cordless knife in a prison in Araraquara, who was there for killing his sister. "He was my friend, but I had to kill," he said.

While in prison at Casa de Custodia in Taubate, Filho would spend four hours a day lifting weights and exercising in his cell, usually between the hours of 5:00 a.m. and 9:00 a.m. "I exercise to defend myself," he said. When he left his cell to enjoy the sunshine in the courtyard, he was always accompanied by two guards, to keep the other prisoners safe.

After serving 34 years, Rodrigues was eventually released from prison in April 2007, only to be rearrested four years later in Balneário Camboriú, in the northeast of Brazil, and sent back to prison for being involved in six riots while in prison and what was termed the "deprivation of liberty."

THE THEORIES

It has been reported Filho killed only men—never women or children—and he claimed there was usually something noble in what motivated him, either revenge or the elimination of those who had harmed others. He once said, "I only kill scoundrels."

"When someone disobeys his code of ethics, he has solutions of his own that do not follow the law," remarked the criminologist Ilana Casoy, who interviewed Filho for her book *Serial Killers: Made in Brazil*. "He was very clear and straightforward. He does not hide behind any inaccurate speech. Despite the crimes, there is one person, Pedro. And Pedro deserves respect, regardless of all the crimes he committed."

In 2018 the killer was released from prison, with the recommendation he did not need any rehabilitation, and has since started a YouTube channel, which at one point had 29,000 subscribers and more than 2.5 million views. He has used his platform to warn young people about the risks of following him. "Crime is no joke," he told newspaper *Folha de Sao Paulo* in 2018. "Many are coming because they see the branches [fame and money], not the root [prison and death]. It's like the Devil: The one hand giveth; the other hand taketh away. There are many young people who come in and when they leave, it is too late." He has almost become a celebrity, who is asked for photographs and to spend time talking with a fascinated public in Brazil. "They know me, but I don't know these people," he has said.

Asked by *Folha de Sao Paulo* if he had killed more than a hundred people, Filho did not deny it. "Come to that, the day when I didn't kill people, I didn't sleep." He added he had no regrets about the murders he had committed.

THE KILLER COUPLE

LOCATION:......GLOUCESTER, ENGLAND, UK

SUSPECTS:...........FRED AND ROSE WEST

VICTIMS:................................11+

DATE:........................1969-94

In January 1994, when police searched a house on Cromwell Street in the English town of Gloucester they found nine mutilated bodies buried beneath the basement and bathroom and in the yard.

The victims had been subjected to sexual abuse and torture before being murdered and dismembered by the married couple Fred and Rose West.

What dark secrets lay behind the front door of this "House of Horrors"?

THE EVENTS

In 1969 a 28-year-old Fred West first met 15-year-old Rose Letts at a bus station in Cheltenham, beginning a union that would see them become the most infamous and sadistic couple of serial killers in British history.

When he met Rose, Fred was living with his daughter Anna Marie and stepdaughter Charmaine in a caravan park, after his first wife Rena Costello had left him. Despite her parents' protestations, Rose, who had spent time in social care, would move into an apartment in Cheltenham with Fred to become his children's nanny. The couple soon moved to a house on Midland Road in Gloucester, and in October 1970 Rose gave birth to their daughter Heather. With Fred imprisoned for six months for theft, a 17-year-old Rose found herself bringing up three girls on her own, and subjected the two eldest to sustained physical violence.

It is believed Rose murdered Charmaine in June 1971, while Fred was still in prison. The girl's body was kept in the coal cellar of Midland Road, before Fred, soon after his release, buried her body in the back yard. Rose explained Charmaine's disappearance by saying she had returned to live with her mother Rena in Scotland. When Rena came looking for her two children, she too was killed, in August 1971. It is believed Fred strangled her in the backseat of a car before burying her in fields near the village of Much Marcle.

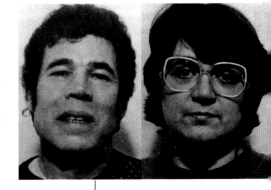

In January 1972 Fred and Rose married at Gloucester Register Office with one guest, Fred's brother John, and in June Rose gave birth to their second child, Mae June. That same year, the couple moved from Midland Road to the now infamous 25 Cromwell Street, the scene for their reign of terror and up to nine murders.

Fred and Rose West pictured here in their mug shots following their arrests in 1994.

The House of Horrors

Rose set herself up as a prostitute in the house, with what she called "Rose's Room," with a red light outside so she would not be disturbed. There were also peepholes so Fred could watch his wife with her clients. The Wests also enjoyed casual sex with some of the lodgers who lived on the upper floors of the house. The pair were sadomasochists who gained pleasure from inflicting pain on their many sexual partners.

By 1983 the eight children in the West household (three were conceived with Rose's clients) were subjected to constant physical and sexual abuse, and it is estimated they required as many as 31 visits to hospital over the course of 20 years. At the age of eight years old, Anna Marie had been raped by her father Fred in the basement, with Rose standing by and watching. When she reached 13, her parents would force her into prostitution, and encouraged her to see clients at their house, with Rose always in the room watching.

The squalid basement at 25 Cromwell Street, where the Wests committed several of their murders.

Between April 1973 and August 1979, the Wests' depravity only increased as they murdered eight young girls at Cromwell Street. The first was 19-year-old Lynda Gough, who was friends with two lodgers at the house and moved in herself in 1973, only to disappear a day later. Her remains would later be found buried under the garage.

Later that year, 15-year-old Carol Ann Cooper disappeared after a night at the cinema with her boyfriend. It is believed she was abducted by Fred in his car and brought to Cromwell Street, where she was raped and tortured before being murdered. Her dismembered body was buried in the basement.

Also in 1973, Lucy Partington, a 21-year-old Exeter University student, was abducted from a bus stop and killed. In 1974, 21-year-old Thérèse Siegenthaler, a Swiss student from south London, was also grabbed from the side of a road as she hitchhiked. That same year, 15-year-old schoolgirl Shirley Hubbard was standing at a bus stop in Droitwich when she was snatched; and in 1975, 18-year-old Juanita Mott, a former lodger, was also killed. Most of these victims were found buried in the basement, with clear evidence they had been suspended from beams in the ceiling while they were abused, many with tape covering their faces and mouths, before they were strangled and buried beneath the floor.

There was a three-year pause in the murder spree until May 1978, when 18-year-old Shirley Robinson, a lodger at the house who was eight months pregnant with Fred's son, was murdered by the pair, with the motive seemingly to remove a potential threat to their marriage rather than the usual sadistic pleasure. The Wests' final murder with a clear sexual motive was believed to have been 17-year-old Alison Chambers in August 1979, who at the time was the couple's nanny. She was found buried in the garden with a belt around her face.

The children talk

In 1986 the Wests' 16-year-old daughter Heather confided in her school friends about her years of sexual and physical violence at the hands of her parents. When they learned this, she was killed by Rose, cut up and buried in the garden underneath the patio, with her siblings told she had left for a job in the seaside resort of Torquay. When Rose told Fred what she had done, he said he felt sick. "I said: 'What on earth did you cut her up for?' She said,

'She wouldn't fit in the dustbin!' Now, the thing that makes it hard, [is] that she cut Heather up and chucked her in a fucking dustbin. Her daughter, in a dustbin."

Six years later, when 13-year-old Louise West told police she had been raped by her father Fred, he was charged with three counts of rape, with Rose as an accomplice, but the trial would collapse when the teenager refused to testify. However, all of the Wests' children were removed from the house and taken into foster care after social services found evidence of abuse.

At this time, the macabre joke among the family was that "Heather was under the patio," and when the foster care staff heard this, they reported it to the police, who gained a search warrant for 25 Cromwell Street on February 24, 1994. Fred quickly confessed to the murder of Heather and said he would lead them to where he had buried her in the garden. There the police found a thighbone and a set of remains that were later identified as Heather, leading to Fred being charged with her murder.

BACKGROUND

Fred was born in to a poor family in Herefordshire in 1941. He witnessed his own sisters being forced to have sex with their father. He struggled at school before leaving at 15 and finding casual work as a farm laborer, truck driver, and ice cream van man. When he met Rose, he had become a disturbed and violent man who had already murdered two teenage girls, one who had been eight months pregnant with his child, and had also been unsuccessfully tried for molesting and raping his own sister years earlier.

Rose had been born in north Devon in 1953, also into a troubled family, with her mother suffering from depression that saw her given electroconvulsive therapy while pregnant, and her father being diagnosed as a paranoid schizophrenic. As a child Rose was raped by her father, and she would in turn molest her two younger brothers Graham and Gordon within the family home. She became a difficult teenager, who saw her parents separate, before grasping the opportunity to escape both of them when she met Fred.

During the search the police found further human remains and ordered an excavation of the entire garden. Fred felt compelled to confess to several murders, and told the police they would find five bodies underneath the basement and one underneath the ground-floor bathroom.

THE THEORIES

Despite Fred initially trying to protect Rose and claim she had no prior knowledge, they had enough evidence to charge both with five counts of murder. Rose continued to claim she was innocent. Fred would eventually be charged with 12 murders, Rose with nine. Within a month Fred would drop his denials and state that Rose had been involved.

Before Fred could be tried he hung himself in his cell at H.M. Prison Birmingham on New Year's Day in 1995. Later that year Rose was convicted of 10 charges of murder at Winchester Crown Court, and was sentenced to life imprisonment without parole.

The Wests were products of their traumatic childhoods, growing up in households marred with incest and sexual abuse. "The first few years of life are extremely important in the development of personality," the forensic psychologist Dr. Julian Boon has said. "In the case of Rose, she was sexually and physically abused by her father. She then hitched up with West, who already was similar in that sort of regard and they had a symbiotic relationship. This meant that they would inevitably become exponential in their common interest, in abusing young girls sexually and in terms of sadism."

2

CELEBRITY MURDERS

Whenever a celebrity is murdered, it grips the world's attention even more than usual. Here we look at some of the most famous cases, including John Lennon being shot on a New York sidewalk, the Playboy Playmate Dorothy Stratten being killed on the brink of global fame, and the Colombian footballer Andrés Escobar being riddled with bullets days after scoring an own goal at the 1994 World Cup.

WIFE

KILLER?

O.J. SIMPSON

LOCATION: .... CALIFORNIA, USA

SUSPECT: .... O.J. SIMPSON

VICTIMS: 2

DATE: .... JUNE 12, 1994

Just after midnight, an Akita dog with bloody feet led neighbors to the front yard of an apartment building, to discover two bodies.

Both Nicole Simpson and Ronald Goldman had been violently stabbed to death within the previous two hours.

Her former husband, O.J. Simpson, soon became the prime suspect, but was he the real killer?

THE EVENTS

In the 1990s O.J. Simpson was one of the most popular celebrities in the United States, who had transformed himself from a sports star to a broadcaster and actor. In 1985 Simpson had married his second wife, Nicole Brown, and they had two children, Sydney and Justin.

It was an unhappy marriage marred by domestic violence, and over the course of its seven years there were a reported 62 incidents of abuse. Simpson pleaded "no contest" to a charge that he had beat his wife in 1989. In 1992 the couple divorced. Nicole alleged O.J. began to stalk her; he once stood outside her house and watched her have sex with her new boyfriend, and would regularly issue threats against her.

On the evening of June 12, 1994, Nicole and O.J. had attended separately their daughter's school dance show. Afterward, Nicole had dined at the restaurant Mezzaluna with her parents and two children before returning

O.J. Simpson married Nicole Brown in 1985, but the couple divorced in 1992 after 62 incidents of domestic abuse.

home. Her mother Juditha realized later she had left her glasses at the restaurant, which Ronald Goldman, a waiter and friend of Nicole, would later take to her when his shift ended that night.

At just after midnight on June 13, the bodies of Nicole and Goldman were found amid a large amount of blood outside her apartment in the Brentwood neighborhood of Los Angeles. They had lain there for two hours. A barefoot Nicole had been stabbed in the head, neck, and hands. Her throat had been slit with such force she had been nearly decapitated. Goldman's body was found beneath a tree next to a fence with similar stab wounds to his body, neck, and hands, and with the envelope containing the glasses he had been returning beside him.

Televised escape

When three Los Angeles detectives attended O.J. Simpson's Rockingham house nearby in Brentwood to inform him of his former wife's murder, they found no sign of him, and most of the property in darkness. Simpson had taken a flight to Chicago earlier that night, but police found blood smeared on the door of his Ford Bronco car parked outside, and when they searched his property's grounds they also found a bloody glove that matched a glove found at the crime scene. When they returned later that morning with a search warrant, they found bloodstains inside the Bronco, and more blood on a pair of socks found inside Simpson's bedroom.

On the morning of June 17, police charged Simpson with two counts of first-degree murder, and arranged for him to surrender by midday, but he attempted to flee the city in his Bronco with his friend Al Cowlings. Most of Simpson's escape was filmed by helicopters hovering overhead that beamed it to an enthralled audience of 95 million. He would drive for around 60 miles (100 km) on the city's freeways before surrendering to police.

It was believed Simpson had been considering committing suicide, as he had left behind a letter which said: "I have had a great life, great friends. Please think of the real O.J. and not this lost person."

```
Name: O.J. Simpson
D.O.B.: July 9, 1947
Description:
Male, 6 ft (185 cm),
dark hair
and eyes
Charge: First-
degree murder,
two counts
```

BACKGROUND

Orenthal James Simpson was born in San Francisco in 1947. He attended the University of Southern California, where he was recognized as the best college football player in the country by winning the Heisman Trophy award. He would enjoy a long and successful professional career in the National Football League (NFL) with the Buffalo Bills between 1969 and 1977, and the San Francisco 49ers between 1978 and 1979. He became the first player to carry the ball for more than 2,000 yards in a season in 1973.

After retiring from playing Simpson became a hugely popular broadcaster and actor, commentating on the NFL, featuring in commercials, and starring in more than 20 movies, including *The Towering Inferno* and *The Naked Gun*.

He once told *The New York Times* his biggest accomplishment in a racially divided United States was that "people looked at me like a man, not a black man."

During his trial, Simpson famously tried on the gloves the murderer had worn to prove they did not fit.

THE THEORIES

In January 1995 Simpson's trial began in downtown Los Angeles and was televised like a real-life soap opera to a gripped worldwide audience. The prosecution argued Nicole's death was the tragic climax of the years of domestic abuse she had suffered at the hands of Simpson, and Goldman had been an unwitting victim when he had returned her mother's glasses. The jury heard Simpson's long history of violence toward his wife, and how in 1989 police responded to panicked calls from her in which she screamed: "He's going to kill me, he's going to kill me!"

Crucially, Simpson did not have an alibi for the night of the murders. Kato Kaelin, his lodger at his Rockingham house, testified he did not see Simpson between 9:36 p.m. and 10:54 p.m., during which time the murders occurred.

It was always assumed the sheer weight of the DNA evidence amassed against Simpson would be enough to gain a conviction. There were 61 drops of blood linking him to the crime, and as the lead prosecutor Marcia Clark famously declared, there was a "trail of blood from the Bundy crime scene through Simpson's Ford Bronco to his bedroom at Rockingham."

The prosecution argued Simpson's DNA was found in blood drops at the crime scene next to bloody footprints, a trail leading away from the victims, inside and outside his Bronco, from the car to his front door at Rockingham, on the bloody glove at his house, and on a pair of socks in his bedroom. The bloody glove also matched the glove found at the crime scene, they were a pair, and the cap also found there had hairs inside matching Simpson's.

Simpson's expensively assembled team of defense lawyers attempted to introduce doubt at every turn, and suggested Simpson was the victim of corrupt policemen and compromised evidence. They argued the DNA evidence could not be relied upon, and that the police had made crucial mistakes in its collection, including wearing dirty gloves, which could have caused contamination.

The defense also claimed the bloody glove at the Rockingham estate had been planted by Mark Fuhrman, the police detective who had found it. When Fuhrman was found to have used racial slurs on tape he had earlier denied using, his credibility was questioned, with racism seen as his motive for framing Simpson.

When Simpson was asked to try on the gloves, he made a big play of showing they didn't fit, even though others testified they could have shrunk after being soaked in so much blood. In the most iconic moment of the trial, one of Simpson's lawyers, Johnny Cochran, gleefully said: "If it doesn't fit, you must acquit!"

On the morning of October 3, 1995, after just four hours of deliberation, the jury acquitted Simpson. In the immediate aftermath of the trial, Simpson promised to find "the real killers," but there have never been any other credible suspects with a motive to kill his former wife or Goldman.

THE MANSON FAMILY
MURDERS

LOCATION: ....CALIFORNIA

SUSPECT: ....CHARLES MANSON

VICTIMS: ....7+

DATE: ....AUGUST 8-10, 1969

Screams and gunshots brought the police to a house on Cielo Drive in the early morning of August 9. The bloody body of a man lay on the lawn—he had been repeatedly stabbed and shot. The body of a woman lay nearby. The word "PIG" was written in blood on the front door. Inside the house were the bodies of the heavily pregnant actress Sharon Tate and hairstylist Jay Sebring. A fifth body was later found outside. The following night, police encountered another grisly murder scene. Leno LaBianca and his wife had been stabbed to death in their Los Feliz home.

Who was behind this horrific murder spree?

THE EVENTS

Sharon Tate was a beautiful 26-year-old movie star who had already appeared in 11 movies and been nominated for a Golden Globe for her role as Jennifer North in *Valley of the Dolls*. She was married to the renowned French-Polish award-winning director Roman Polanski, who on the fateful night was away filming in London.

On the evening of August 8, 1969, Tate was eight and a half months pregnant and at home at 10050 Cielo Drive, in the Benedict Canyon area of Los Angeles, with three friends: hairstylist Jay Sebring, screenwriter Wojciech Frykowski, and Abigail Folger, who was heiress to the Folger coffee empire. Meanwhile, Manson ordered four of his followers, Tex Watson, Susan Atkins, Linda Kasabian, and Patricia Krenwinkel, to go to Tate's house and "totally destroy" everyone there and do it "as gruesome as you can."

This group arrived at the house just after midnight, cut the telephone lines, then shot and killed their first victim, 18-year-old Steven Parent, who was driving out of the property after visiting its caretaker William Garretson.

Watson entered the house through a window before letting Atkins and Krenwinkel through the front door. Frykowski was asleep on a sofa in the living room, and after waking him with a violent kick to the head, Watson chillingly said, "I'm the devil, and I'm here to do the devil's business."

Meanwhile, Atkins and Krenwinkel rounded up Tate, Folger, and Sebring from other parts of the house and forced them into the living room.

Actress Sharon Tate was one of the Manson Family's victims.

Watson joined together Tate and Sebring with a rope around their necks and threw it over a beam, as if he was set to hang them both. Sebring pleaded for mercy for the heavily pregnant Tate, which prompted Watson to pull out a gun and shoot him before stabbing him seven times.

The horror continued to unfold with Frykowski freeing himself from the towel that had been tied around his hands and making a run for his life out of the front door—but Watson followed him, and shot and stabbed him. On the front lawn he was finally killed with a total of 51 stab wounds and multiple blows to the head with the butt of a gun. Folger would also make an escape to the pool area of the house, but Krenwinkel caught her, and along with Watson, stabbed her 28 times.

"Horrifying sounds"

The group's lookout, Kasabian, heard "horrifying sounds" and came for a closer look. "I saw a woman in a white dress [Tate] and she had blood all over her and she was screaming and she was calling for her mom. I saw Katie [Krenwinkel] stabbing her," she said in court. "I thought about going to a house where there were lights down the road and then I said, 'No, don't do that, because they'll find me and kill all those people.' So I went down the hill and I got into the car and I just stayed there and waited."

Tate would become the fifth and final victim of the night when her pleas to save her and her unborn child's lives were ruthlessly ignored, and she was killed with as many as 16 stab wounds.

Manson had instructed his team of followers to "leave something witchy, a sign to let the world know you were there," and so Atkins collected some of Tate's blood and used it to write "Pig" in large letters on the white front door.

The followers made their escape by car, and as they drove off, Kasabian took the weapons from each of them before tossing them into a local ravine.

```
Name:
Charles Manson
D.O.B.:
November 12, 1934
Description: Male,
5 ft 2 in. (157 cm),
dark hair and eyes
Charge: Murder,
9 counts
```

SO VENTURA CAL
47 6 2 3

BACKGROUND

During the late Sixties, a drifter and part-time musician Charles Manson came to lead a cult known as the Manson Family from a southern Californian ranch.

Manson was an ex-convict who had spent most of his life in prison for petty crimes, but managed to lure in a vulnerable group of up to 100 young people who were willing to follow his every command.

According to the former Los Angeles District Attorney Vincent Bugliosi, who would successfully prosecute Manson for the subsequent murders, Manson was highly intelligent, despite being uneducated, and had the ability to gain control over other people and get them to do terrible things. He went on to say, "Eventually [Manson] convinced them that he was the second coming: Christ and the Devil all wrapped up in the same person." This helped Manson force his followers to commit murder in his name when they took part in a horrific spree of crimes in the summer of 1969.

Sharon Tate's body was removed from her rented house on Cielo Drive in the Bel Air Estates area of Los Angeles on the morning of August 9, 1969.

THE THEORIES

Why Manson inspired his followers to commit seven murders of innocent people they barely knew with such horrific sadism is a question that has been relentlessly debated in the 50 years since the crimes.

One theory is Manson, as a white supremacist, wanted to spark a race war all across America by suggesting the murders were committed by black Americans or even the Black Panthers. He referred to this race war as "Helter Skelter," inspired by the lyrics of a Beatles song, which in his warped mind he believed predicted this clash. Once a race war began, he would retreat to an underground city with his followers before emerging in the aftermath to rule over the black population.

Manson was also a musician who would come close to gaining fame in the late Sixties, but his ultimate rejection only stoked his anger. He first became friends with Dennis Wilson from the Beach Boys, who would record one of his songs, but when it was released the band had changed the title, the tempo of the song, and refused to give him a writing credit. For this perceived betrayal, Manson threatened to murder Wilson. Around the same time, Manson also met Terry Melcher, a record producer who was the son of the Hollywood legend Doris Day, and was hopeful he would give him a recording contract. Melcher was dating the rising young actress Candice Bergen, who was renting the house at 10050 Cielo Drive, the scene of the murders, where Manson and Wilson would become frequent guests. Melcher would enrage Manson by ultimately deciding not to help him with his musical career, and in January 1969 he and Bergen moved out of the property. On the night of the murders in August that year, Manson was fully aware that Melcher no longer lived there, but consumed with a warped vengeance, the house had become a symbol of his rejection by the Hollywood elite and he wanted to kill everyone who now lived there. Manson also hoped the murders would scare Melcher and serve as some form of misguided revenge for his rejection.

Despite serving life in prison for his terrible crimes, Manson neither confirmed or denied these theories before his death in California State Prison on November 19, 2017.

DEATH

ON THE

SIDEWALK

LOCATION:..........................NEW YORK, USA

SUSPECT:.........................MARK CHAPMAN

VICTIM:............................JOHN LENNON

DATE:.....................DECEMBER 8, 1980

On a cold December night in 1980, five shots pierced the air outside The Dakota building on New York's Upper West Side before a fatally wounded John Lennon slumped to the floor.

Deranged fan Mark Chapman had approached Lennon at the building's entrance and fired these shots into the musician's back with a powerful Charter Arms .38-caliber pistol.

Twenty-five minutes later, the beloved former member of the Beatles was pronounced dead on arrival at the city's Roosevelt Hospital, causing an outpouring of grief that reverberated around the world.

Why was the music legend murdered in cold blood?

THE EVENTS

At the start of the 1980s, John Lennon was revered as both a musical icon and a political activist, with a legion of devoted fans all over the world. After first enjoying fame in the Beatles alongside Paul McCartney, Ringo Starr, and George Harrison during the 1960s, Lennon went on to forge a hugely successful solo career, selling over 28 million albums. The Liverpudlian had moved to New York in 1971, where at the time of his death he lived with his wife Yoko Ono and their five-year-old son Sean.

On December 8, 1980, Lennon had spent the morning doing a photo shoot for *Rolling Stone* magazine in his seventh-floor apartment at The Dakota before leaving in the afternoon to record music at The Record Plant studio. At around 5:00 p.m., as Lennon and Ono walked to a waiting limousine to take them to the studio, he signed autographs and posed for photographs for the groups of fans who would often be waiting outside. There, on the sidewalk, Lennon signed a copy of his new album *Double Fantasy* for Mark Chapman, a fan who just hours later would take his life.

The entrance to The Dakota on Manhattan's Upper West Side, opposite Central Park.

Name: Mark Chapman
D.O.B.: May 10, 1955
Description: Male,
5 ft 10 in. (178 cm),
dark hair and eyes
Charge: Second-
degree murder

BACKGROUND

Mark Chapman was born in Fort Worth, Texas, in 1955, and raised in Georgia by his father David, a sergeant in the US Air Force, and mother Diane.

After spells working in various Chicago churches, and then with Vietnamese refugees in Arkansas for the charity World Vision, Chapman moved to Hawaii and took a job as a printer in Honolulu's Castle Memorial Hospital in 1977.

By December 1980 he was 25 years old and had married Gloria Abe, but was unemployed, having recently resigned from a job as a security guard. He had no criminal convictions, and it is understood he had never used a gun before he decided to stalk and murder John Lennon. However, Chapman had long suffered with mental illness and clinical depression, and in 1977 had failed with a suicide attempt. Not long before the murder, he had diagnosed himself as a schizophrenic.

Lennon and Ono pictured
in New York in 1980,
Lennon's final year
of life.

Chapman would wait there in the shadows of the building's archway for another six hours until Lennon returned from the studio.

At 10:50 p.m. Lennon and Ono pulled up in a limousine and walked toward the building, where they passed Chapman. There were reports Lennon briefly glanced at Chapman and recognized him from earlier, before seconds later, Chapman pulled a gun from his pocket and fired five shots at Lennon's back.

One shot missed and shattered a window in The Dakota, but the other four hit Lennon in the back and shoulder, puncturing his lung and severing an artery to his heart, causing him to bleed heavily from the wounds, and his mouth.

"I'm shot, I'm shot!" Lennon shouted as he staggered into the building's reception and fell to the floor. A concierge at The Dakota Jay Hastings attended to Lennon and called the police. At least six police officers quickly arrived on the scene, where they found Chapman standing patiently on the sidewalk, next to the still-hot revolver he had dropped and holding a copy of J.D. Salinger's *The Catcher in the Rye*.

The killer made no attempts to resist arrest before he had handcuffs placed on him and was put in the back of a police car.

The officers found Lennon lying facedown in a pool of blood in the reception area, and seeing the severity of his injuries, realized they could not wait for an ambulance, but instead one of them carried Lennon to the backseat of a police car to transport him to hospital. The officer James Moran asked, "Are you John Lennon?", to which the victim struggled to nod and reply "Yes."

In the days after his death, distraught fans left flowers and messages for Lennon at the scene of the crime.

Moran arrived at the Roosevelt Hospital, 13 blocks south of The Dakota building, at around 11:00 p.m., carrying Lennon on his back and pleading for help, but Lennon at that point was no longer breathing and had no pulse. A medical team worked on Lennon for around 10 minutes in an effort to resuscitate him, but it was to no avail and he was declared dead at 11:15 p.m. A coroner's report would later state he had lost more than 80 percent of his blood.

The following day, Ono declared there would be no funeral for Lennon, just a private cremation, and instead, on December 14, she held a 10-minute silence for him, attended by over 225,000 people in New York's Central Park.

THE THEORIES

What possessed Chapman to travel from his home in Hawaii to casually murder John Lennon in front of his wife on that New York sidewalk?

One theory is Chapman, who had been a committed Beatles fan as a teenager, had become enraged at Lennon's frivolous comment made in 1966 that the band was becoming "more popular than Jesus." As a born-again Christian, it is believed this had particularly upset him.

His anger had also been fueled by his perception Lennon was not staying true to his beliefs, singing about just needing love and no possessions while at the same time living the indulgent lifestyle of a multimillionaire.

"When I got angry at Lennon, I found a book in the library that showed him on the roof of The Dakota, it's a very nice, sumptuous building," Chapman explained in an interview in 1992. "And, remember I'm in a different state of mind and I'm falling in on myself, and I'm angry at seeing him on The Dakota and I say to myself, that phony, that bastard. And I got that mad. I took the book home to my wife and I said, 'Look, he's a phony.' It started with anger."

The *Catcher in the Rye* connection

Chapman taking a copy of J.D. Salinger's 1951 novel *The Catcher in the Rye* with him to murder Lennon has always been highly relevant. He had written inside the cover, "This is my statement," and signed it Holden Caulfield. In the novel, the leading character Holden Caulfield is angered by adults who are "phonies," falsely portraying themselves as something they are not; a view Chapman increasingly empathized with, citing Lennon as a prime example.

When he was arrested at the scene of the crime, Chapman was keen to tell the police why he was holding a copy of this book:

"On December 8, 1980, Mark David Chapman was a very confused person," he has said about himself. "He was literally living inside of a paperback novel, J.D. Salinger's *The Catcher in the Rye*.

"I'm not blaming a book. I blame myself for crawling inside of the book and I certainly want to say that J.D. Salinger and *The Catcher in the Rye* didn't cause me to kill John Lennon. I feel badly about that. It's my fault. I crawled in, found my pseudo-self within these pages...and played out the whole thing."

In August 1981, Chapman was sentenced to 20 years to life for the second-degree murder of Lennon, and by 2021, at the age of 66, he remained incarcerated, having been denied parole on 11 separate occasions.

CASE CLOSED

PLAYBOY
PLAYMATE
DEATH

LOCATION: ....LOS ANGELES, USA

SUSPECT: ....PAUL SNIDER

VICTIM: ....DOROTHY STRATTEN

DATE: ....AUGUST 14, 1980

"The happiest girl in the world" is how Dorothy Stratten described herself in the spring of 1980. The beautiful 20-year-old Canadian model already enjoyed fame as a Playboy Playmate and was on the verge of becoming a major movie star.

But in the August of that same year, she was lured to a house in West Los Angeles and murdered by her estranged husband Paul Snider, who then committed suicide by turning the shotgun on himself.

"It looked like it was a horror movie" is how Snider's roommate described the scene when she discovered the two blood-splattered bodies lying on the floor of Snider's bedroom.

Why was Stratten's promising life cut so tragically short?

THE EVENTS

In 1977 Dorothy Stratten was a 17-year-old high-school student working at a Dairy Queen in her native Vancouver when a 26-year-old Paul Snider walked in to her ice cream store and was immediately struck by her beauty. Snider would later persuade her to pose for a series of nude pictures he would then send to *Playboy* magazine as they searched for new models to feature in their forthcoming 25th anniversary issue.

"You think of [Snider] and you think of a wolf, and you think of him stalking his prey," the actress Mariel Hemingway has said, who would play Stratten in the 1983 movie about her life, *Star 80*.

Playboy believed they had discovered a star when they saw the set of pictures and immediately invited Stratten to Los Angeles, where she was featured in the magazine and named Playmate of the Month for August 1979. In that same year, Stratten married Snider, against the wishes of her friends. "He pushed her into marrying him, I don't think she really wanted to," Alison Reynolds, the former social secretary of *Playboy*, has said.

Stratten met Snider when she was working behind the counter of a Dairy Queen in Vancouver.

Stratten with the Playboy
publisher Hugh Hefner,
after she became the
magazine's Playmate of
the Month for August 1979.

It would not be long before Stratten began to resent Snider's jealousy and controlling tendencies. "I think he really thought, 'This is mine,'" Hemingway has added. "He wanted ownership of her. He wanted to say that he owned something, that he did something...I think he thought he made her."

Stratten's appearances in *Playboy* gave her the opportunity to move more into acting, and she had some minor parts on the television series *Fantasy Island* and *Buck Rogers in the 25th Century*, and in the low-budget movies *Americathon*, *Skatetown USA,* and *Galaxina*.

The iconic *Playboy* publisher Hugh Hefner had helped to undermine Snider's influence over Stratten by providing her with a new manager and accountant. Stratten was also introduced to the director Peter Bogdanovich, who quickly cast her in his forthcoming movie *They All Laughed*, and soon after filming commenced, the pair began an affair.

In June 1980 Stratten wrote to Snider telling him she believed their marriage was over, before going on a 10-day holiday to England with Bogdanovich. On their return she moved in to his mansion in the Bel Air district of Los Angeles. Snider flew into a rage, hiring a detective to follow Stratten, and even sold some of her belongings, including a Jaguar she had been given by *Playboy*.

On the night of July 31, 1980, Snider hid in the bushes outside Bogdanovich's mansion armed with a handgun, but after several hours, when no one appeared, he grew bored and left.

Eight days later, Stratten and Snider met each other for the first time in three months at the West Los Angeles house they used to share. Snider's hopes of a reconciliation were thwarted by both Stratten's declaration of love for Bogdanovich and her insistence that she saw her future with the director.

A final meeting

The following week on August 14, the pair met at the same venue to negotiate and finalize the details of their separation. Bogdanovich and a host of Stratten's friends asked her not to see Snider, but she hoped they could remain friends, and believed she was never in any danger. At noon, Stratten arrived in her green Mercury Cougar and entered the house for the meeting. There was evidence the couple spent some time in the living room, because Stratten's purse was found there, before they went to Snider's bedroom.

Bogdanovich directed Stratten in They All Laughed, and soon became her lover.

Snider was then sharing the house with two friends, Stephen Cushner and Patti Laurman, who were out when Stratten arrived. On their return, they had noticed her car was still outside, and so assumed the couple had reconciled and were together in Snider's bedroom. After watching television for several hours together, Cushner and Laurman were aware of how quiet the rest of the house seemed, and how Snider had not answered his phone when it had rung, and so, at around 11:00 p.m., they went to investigate by knocking on the bedroom door.

There was no answer, but the two friends pushed it open to find Stratten and Snider both naked and dead. "It looked like it was a horror movie, a staged horror movie, like mannequins and fake blood," Laurman said. "That's a picture that never goes away, a mental picture that's stuck in here forever."

The police later ascertained Stratten had been raped then shot in the face by Snider with a 12-gauge shotgun around an hour after she had arrived at the house, before he pointed the gun at his own face and pulled the trigger.

CASE CLOSED

Snider cuts
a cake with
Stratten as they
celebrate her
20th birthday
in 1980.

BACKGROUND

Paul Snider was born into a Jewish family in the Canadian city of Vancouver in April 1951. During the 1970s he had made a career for himself as a promoter of car and cycling shows, but would also supplement his income as a pimp. He was not shy about how he earned his money, and could be seen around Vancouver driving a Corvette and wearing a mink coat, an open-neck shirt, and extravagant jewels hung around his neck.

When Snider walked into that Dairy Queen, he immediately saw Stratten as both his meal ticket and route to the big time, so years later, when she ended their marriage, he saw his income drain away—and simmered with rage.

"Paul was distraught," his former roommate Laurman told ABC in 2019. "He was sad. He was like, 'Gosh. She didn't even tell me she loved me or kiss me.' There were times when he talked to me and he would start crying. He would sit on the couch and play his guitar, and wrote songs to Dorothy."

THE DEATH OF
FASHION

LOCATION:...........................MIAMI, USA

SUSPECT:.....................ANDREW CUNANAN

VICTIM:......................GIANNI VERSACE

DATE:...........................JULY 15, 1997

On the steps of his palatial mansion on a busy street opposite Miami Beach, one of the world's most famous fashion designers, Gianni Versace, was brutally killed with two shots to the back of his head.

This proved to be Andrew Cunanan's fifth and final victim in a horrific murder spree that took him across the United States over the course of three months.

What had motivated Cunanan to murder Versace and four other men?

THE EVENTS

By the summer of 1997 Gianni Versace was one of the most famous and beloved names in the global fashion industry. After opening his first boutique in Milan, in his native Italy, in 1978, he was hailed for his bold and vibrant designs and spectacular use of color. Over the next two decades he would open up to 130 boutiques around the world, selling dresses worth up to $30,000, as he built up a business empire worth over $800 million.

Versace first fell in love with Miami in 1992 and decided to settle in the city, buying a three-story mansion on Ocean Drive, opposite Miami Beach, for $2.9 million. "The mood is very, very easy [here]," Versace told the *Miami Herald* in 1993. "That is special, and I don't find the mood any place else in the world."

When he stayed at his mansion, Versace had a regular routine every morning of walking the three blocks to the News Café, where he would purchase some magazines, or sometimes sit at a table and enjoy an orange juice. On that fateful morning in July 1997, Versace followed this routine, leaving his mansion at around 8:30 a.m. and, wearing a white tee, black shorts, and

The steps of Versace's Ocean Drive mansion opposite Miami Beach, where he was murdered.

sandals, strolled to the News Café, where he spent $15 on five magazines including *Vogue*, *People*, and *The New Yorker*.

Versace returned home just before 9:00 a.m., and as he went to open his front gates, a man carrying a backpack sprung forward from the sidewalk and fired two shots from a .40-caliber handgun into the back of his head.

From a nearby skating shop, Eddie Bianchi was an eyewitness to the shooting. "We were right there watching and there's nothing you can do," he told *The New York Times*. "His blood was coming out like crazy. He shook a little bit and stopped moving."

Versace's partner, Antonio D'Amico, was sipping a cup of coffee inside the mansion when he heard the shots outside. "The house had stained-glass windows so we couldn't see what had happened from inside, so we had to open the gate," he told the *Guardian* in 2017. "I saw Gianni lying on the steps, with blood around him. At that point, everything went dark. I was pulled away, I didn't see any more."

Versace was rushed to hospital, but at 9:15 a.m. was pronounced dead on arrival at the Jackson Memorial Hospital Ryder Trauma Center.

Medical examiners removed Cunanan's body after he committed suicide on a houseboat in Miami.

WANTED BY THE FBI

Taken about April 1997

Andrew Cunanan

© FBI   Supplied by ONLINE USA

Andrew Cunanan, a 27-year-old drifter, quickly emerged as the main suspect for the murder, as the FBI had already been tracking him for the deaths of four men in the space of just 12 days in April and May earlier that year. Even though Cunanan was on the FBI's Most Wanted list, he had managed to evade them for more than two months, and since the start of May had been living in an apartment in Miami 4 miles (6.5 km) from Versace's mansion.

Eyewitnesses to the shooting were able to clearly describe Cunanan and what he was wearing when he shot Versace: a gray tee, black shorts, and a white cap, which were found by police in a garage next to a red Chevrolet 1995 pickup truck he had stolen from his fourth murder victim William Reese. Cunanan's image was plastered on Wanted posters all over Miami as the police and FBI closed in, with over 1,000 agents involved across the country.

On July 23, nine days after Versace's death, a caretaker discovered that Cunanan was hiding out on a luxury houseboat on Miami's Indian Creek canal. According to police, in the days after the murder, the suspect had been urgently trying to organize a counterfeit passport to flee the country, but had been unable to secure one. "He was a desperate person with very little room to move about," Miami Beach Police Chief Richard Barreto said.

As a police assault team began to surround the houseboat, Cunanan sat on a bed inside and committed suicide by shooting himself in the head with the same gun he had fired to kill Gianni Versace.

THE THEORIES

When police found Cunanan's body, they were frustrated to discover he had failed to leave a suicide note, which in the years since has only served to fuel the theories about why he murdered Versace.

It has never been firmly established whether Cunanan and Versace had previously known each other, but there have been reports they first met at the San Francisco nightclub Colossus on the night of October 21, 1990. *Vanity Fair* reported that eyewitnesses remember Versace seemingly recognizing Cunanan there, and saying, "I know you, Lago di Como, no?" Cunanan was flattered he had remembered him. However, there has never been any evidence Cunanan had ever been to Versace's house on Lake Como, in Italy, but it was known Versace would often use that line when he wished to strike up conversation with someone.

A friend of Cunanan's called Doug Stubblefield has been quoted as saying he later saw Cunanan and Versace traveling in a large chauffeured car along Market Street in San Francisco. Could it be that Cunanan harbored feelings for Versace and the murder was an act of revenge for an unknown slight? However, the Versace family have always vehemently denied that Gianni had ever met or knew his killer.

BACKGROUND

Andrew Cunanan was born in National City, California, in 1969, the youngest of four children, to Navy veteran Modesto and his wife Mary Anne. As a child Cunanan was exceptionally bright, with an IQ of 147, but he was also a pathological liar and a fantasist, who told false stories to impress, including that his father was an Israeli millionaire, his family had amassed a fortune with a pineapple plantation business, and they knew the First Lady of the Philippines Imelda Marcos.

After dropping out of college, Cunanan, who always had a fascination with the rich and famous, funded an extravagant lifestyle by dating a succession of wealthy older men. There have also been reports he was a male prostitute.

A bid for fame, or a case of revenge?

Bill Hagmaier, a former chief at the FBI, has suggested Versace was "the wealthy, high-profile homosexual success story that Andrew Cunanan was never going to be," and the only way Cunanan could ever have the fame he craved was to kill him.

"The world would know two things after the murder of Gianni Versace," former FBI criminal profiler Candice DeLong told ABC News. "One, they would know who Versace was. And two, they would know his killer was Andrew Cunanan. That's what Andrew wanted. 'Look at me. I can get to anyone.'"

One loose theory is that Cunanan believed he had been infected with HIV and wanted to gain revenge on who he thought might have given it to him, including his first victim Jeff Trail, who he murdered in Minneapolis in April. But Trail's family have said while he was friends with Cunanan, they had never been in a relationship, and to add to the mystery an autopsy of Cunanan revealed he had not been HIV positive.

Investigators are still at a loss to understand what triggered a killing spree that would leave five men dead over the course of less than three months, which included Jeff Trail and David Madson in Minnesota, Lee Miglin in Chicago, William Reese in New Jersey, and finally Gianni Versace in Miami.

FROM
HERO TO
MURDERER

LOCATION:.......PRETORIA, SOUTH AFRICA

SUSPECT:....................OSCAR PISTORIUS

VICTIM:.....................REEVA STEENKAMP

DATE:.....................FEBRUARY 14, 2013

Screams and gunshots rang out in the middle of the night at an exclusive housing community in the South African city of Pretoria.

The police were called to the scene, where they found the body of model Reeva Steenkamp riddled with bullets, with her boyfriend, the Paralympian and national hero Oscar Pistorius, weeping beside her. Pistorius immediately confessed he had shot Steenkamp as he believed she was a burglar and they were both under threat.

Was he telling the truth or was he guilty of her murder?

THE EVENTS

Reeva Steenkamp was a beautiful 29-year-old South African model who, at the start of 2013, was becoming famous for her appearances on the cover of men's magazines, and for advertising Avon, KFC, and Toyota. Since November 2012 she had been in a relationship with the Paralympian sprinter Oscar Pistorius, a gold-medal winner at the recent London 2012 games, who was feted across the world as a role model and an inspiration.

The new couple had spent the evening of February 13, 2013, together at Pistorius's house on the high-security, gated Silver Woods Country Estate, and at 10:00 p.m., according to Pistorius, Reeva was doing yoga exercises and he was watching television in bed, with his prosthetic legs removed.

Pistorius kept a 9-mm Parabellum pistol underneath his bed every night as he was concerned about intruders breaking into his house during the night, even though that night he also slept with his balcony doors open.

The seemingly golden couple, Steenkamp and Pistorius, at the South African Sports Awards in November 2012.

At around 3:00 a.m., Pistorius says he got up to close the doors, and heard a noise and movement coming from his bedroom's en suite bathroom. Without attaching his prosthetic legs or switching on the bedroom's lights, he grabbed his pistol and went to investigate.

An intruder?

"It filled me with horror and fear of an intruder or intruders being inside the toilet," Pistorius would later explain in his affidavit. "I thought he or they must have entered through the unprotected window. As I did not have my prosthetic legs on and felt extremely vulnerable, I knew I had to protect Reeva and myself. I felt trapped as my bedroom door was locked and I have limited mobility on my stumps. I fired shots at the toilet door and shouted to Reeva to phone the police. She did not respond."

When Pistorius realized his girlfriend was not in their bed, he tried to open the bathroom door, but realizing it was locked, grabbed a cricket bat and broke it down with force, finding her bloodied body slumped on the floor.

Steenkamp had been crouching behind the locked door, and according to a pathologist who would later inspect her, she had been killed by a fatal shot to the head, and also been hit in the arm and pelvis.

Pistorius called an ambulance and carried Steenkamp down the staircase, where he attempted to perform mouth-to-mouth resuscitation on her.

A neighbor in the community, a doctor called Johan Stipp, had rushed to the scene to attend to Steenkamp, but found on arrival she had no pulse, no signs of breathing, and dilated pupils, and he confirmed she was dead. The police arrived to find Steenkamp's bloodied body covered in towels at the bottom of the staircase, while Pistorius, with his prosthetic legs now attached, was in his garage with blood on his clothes, holding his head and crying.

Pistorius
wins the gold
medal for the
200m T44 at the
2012 London
Paralympics.

BACKGROUND

Oscar Pistorius was born in 1986 without fibula bones and had to have both legs amputated below the knees when he was 11 months old. He refused to be burdened by his disability and would go on to become one of the world's most recognizable sports people, appearing in both disability and nondisability sporting competitions against able-bodied athletes.

Pistorius became known as the "Blade Runner" or "the fastest man on no legs" for competing in races with prosthetic blades attached to his stumps. He would amass a total haul of six gold medals, one silver, and one bronze across three Paralympic Games in Athens 2004, Beijing 2008, and London 2012 at the T44 level for distances between 100 meters and 400 meters. He also became the first amputee to win a nondisabled world track medal with his part in the South African 4 x 400 relay team at the 2011 World Championships in Daegu. Pistorius had fans and sponsors flocking to him—until his arrest for Steenkamp's death in February 2013.

THE THEORIES

An hour after Steenkamp was shot, Hilton Botha, an experienced detective with the South African Police Service attended the house and asked Pistorius what had happened. "I thought it was a burglar," was his reply. This was the Paralympian sprinter's immediate explanation and he stuck to it throughout many hours of police interviews and the various court cases that followed.

The heavily guarded suspect leaves the High Court in Pretoria, South Africa, in October 2014.

Yet Pistorius's account also raised many questions: Why would a burglar lock himself inside a bathroom? Why didn't Pistorius find out where Steenkamp was before he started firing? Why hadn't he simply made sure his girlfriend was safe and fled from the bedroom?

According to Botha, the bullets hit Steenkamp on her right side, which suggested she had not been sitting on the toilet but crouching behind the door, possibly in fear, before she died. She was also found with her cell phone, which seemed strange that she would take it with her for a quick trip to the bathroom in the middle of the night. Botha also examined the bullets on the floor of the bathroom, and believed that the holes in the door had a downward trajectory, suggesting Pistorius had been wearing his prosthetic legs when he fired the shots.

Botha did not believe Pistorius's story and thought this was a simple and obvious case of murder. "There is no way anything else could have happened," he told *Vanity Fair* in 2013. "It was just them in the house, and according to the security registers she had been staying there for two to three days, so he had to be used to her by that time. There was no forced entry. The only place there could have been entrance was the open bathroom window, and we did everything we could to see if anyone went through it, and it was impossible. So I thought it was an open-and-closed case. He shot her, that's it. I was convinced that it was murder."

Anger issues

Pistorius had cultivated an image of a clean-cut sporting hero who had overcome adversity, but in the aftermath of Steenkamp's death, a series of troubling stories emerged that showed he had a history of anger issues. Most notably, in 2009 he had been arrested for assault for allegedly slamming a door on a woman, Cassidy Taylor-Memmory, during a party—so hard that the door shattered and injured her. Pistorius denied the charge, which would later be dropped, before he entered into settlement negotiations with her.

At his trial in 2014, Pistorius was found not guilty of murder but guilty of culpable homicide, and received a five-year prison sentence. However, in 2015 the Supreme Court of Appeal of South Africa overturned the verdict and convicted him of murder, with his sentence being extended to six years. The National Prosecuting Authority appealed the leniency of this sentence, which was eventually increased to 13 years and 5 months. Pistorius will be eligible for parole from 2023.

THE
COLOMBIAN
SOCCER MURDER

LOCATION: ....MEDELLÍN, COLOMBIA

VICTIM: ....ANDRÉS ESCOBAR

DATE: ....JULY 2, 1994

The captain of the Colombian national soccer team, Andrés Escobar, was found slumped dead behind his steering wheel in the parking lot of a Medellín nightclub after being riddled with six bullets by a gunman.

Only nine days earlier, the captain had scored a damaging own goal in his country's 2–1 defeat to the USA, which had pushed the Colombian team to the verge of being knocked out of the World Cup finals.

Was Escobar killed as an act of revenge for his mistake on the field?

THE EVENTS

Colombia arrived at the 1994 World Cup finals in the USA with the unusual status as one of the favorites to win the tournament. There was an expectation they could become world champions for the first time ever; a view supported by one of the game's greatest ever players, Pelé.

By the summer of 1994, Colombia had lost just one of their previous 26 games, and in the qualifiers had conquered their fierce South American rivals Argentina 5–0, who had reached the final of the two previous World Cups.

There was a fervent hope in Colombia that any success their national soccer team enjoyed would help bring together a country scarred by the violent drug wars that had been waged for nearly three decades. Following the death of the infamous drug lord Pablo Escobar (no relation to Andrés) in December 1993, these wars had spun further out of control, with an increase in shootings, bombings, and kidnaps.

"When Pablo Escobar died, the earth shook and the wind cried 'Pablo Escobar!'" Colombia's manager Francisco Maturana has said. "As of that moment, you had to be on guard at all times. You couldn't trust anyone. Even a policeman could be good or evil."

The World Cup trophy is 18-carat gold, and this version has been awarded to the winners since 1974.

Escobar scored his infamous own goal in a 2-1 defeat to the USA at the 1994 World Cup finals.

Unfortunately, the Colombian team were unable to provide solace to their troubled homeland; the expectations would prove to be too heavy, and they lost their opening World Cup game 3–1 to Romania.

"That marked the beginning of a psychological crisis for which the team wasn't prepared," the journalist César Mauricio Velásquez told the *Guardian*. "Many gamblers lost big money and there appeared a sort of 'dark hand' that was upset with the team's performance."

In Colombia's second group game, with a win needed to remain in the tournament, their captain, Escobar, scored an own goal in a 2–1 defeat to the hosts.

Colombia would rally in their third and final group game to beat Switzerland 2–0, but it was too little, too late, and they were forced to leave the World Cup earlier than expected, with a deep sense of disappointment.

Escobar was upset by Colombia's failure, but felt it was important to project a message of unity and calm. He wrote a column in Bogotá's *El Tiempo* newspaper: "Life doesn't end here. We have to go on. No matter how difficult, we must stand back up. We only have two options: either allow anger to paralyze us and the violence continues, or we overcome and try our best to help others. It's our choice. Let us please maintain respect."

Back in his hometown of Medellín, the epicenter of Colombia's drug wars, Escobar was aware he might become a target for violence. His manager Maturana preached caution, telling Escobar, "Here conflicts aren't resolved with fists. Andrés, stay at home. But Andrés said, 'No, I must show my face to my people.'"

A fatal night out

On the evening of July 2, despite knowing the risks involved, Escobar decided to venture out for the first time since his return from the World Cup in the USA, and arranged to meet friends at a local nightclub. At Medellín's El Indio bar, the evening started calmly, with Escobar and his friends enjoying some drinks. Escobar was instantly recognized by most of the other cutomers, but the chat was at first good natured and supportive.

This would soon turn into abuse, with some at the bar mocking Escobar for his own goal, forcing him to leave. He was followed by a group of men into the parking lot, with some eyewitnesses recalling him being called a "faggot." Escobar got into his car and attempted to reason with the group, when one of them suddenly produced a gun and fired six bullets into him, which saw him slump onto his steering wheel. An ambulance was brought to the scene, but Escobar was already dead.

In the following days, Escobar's body would be on display in a wooden casket at a local basketball arena, where over 100,000 Colombians took the opportunity to pay their respects before his funeral, where another 15,000 were in attendance as he was laid to rest.

THE THEORIES

On the night of the murder, eyewitnesses gave police a license plate number for one of the vehicles that had fled the scene, which was believed to have contained some of the men who had confronted Escobar. It was traced to Pedro and Juan Gallón, renowned local drug traffickers who had previously worked for Pablo Escobar before moving to a rival gang.

However, it was their bodyguard Humberto Castro Munoz who would confess to the murder of Escobar and be sentenced to 43 years in prison, later reduced to 26 years. He was eventually released after serving only 11 years. The Gallóns were cleared of any wrongdoing.

The assumption has always been gangsters who had lost money betting on Colombia at the World Cup killed Escobar as an act of revenge, but this has never been definitively proven.

"The wrong end of the stick"?

The Colombian manager at the 1994 World Cup, Maturana, has dismissed the notion Escobar was killed because of his own goal. "People get the wrong end of the stick," he has said. "You have to remember that it was a difficult time for Colombia as a country. It was a social thing, nothing to do with sport. When it happened there were people who wanted to link it to something, to say it was because of the World Cup. But it wasn't! It was an argument that any Colombian person could have had at a time of a lot of intolerance, a time when people didn't talk, but fought instead. And they didn't use their fists either. The first thing they did was pull out a gun. And Andrés had the misfortune of being in the wrong place at the wrong time."

ANDRES ESCOBAR
1967 - 1994

BACKGROUND

Born in 1967, Andrés Escobar became known as one of Colombia's greatest defenders, hailed as "El Caballero del Futbol," ("the Gentleman of Soccer"). He made his professional debut for his hometown club Atlético Nacional in 1986, and would play a total of 238 games for them, in between a season playing for Young Boys in Switzerland. He would also make 51 appearances for the Colombian national team, and captain them to the 1994 World Cup finals in the USA.

In that same year, Escobar had an offer to join the reigning European champions AC Milan after the tournament, and was also due to marry his fiancée Pamela Cascardo.

THE ASSASSINATION OF ROBERT F. KENNEDY

LOCATION: .... LOS ANGELES, USA

SUSPECT: .... SIRHAN SIRHAN

VICTIMS: .... ROBERT F. KENNEDY

DATE: .... JUNE 5, 1968

Robert F. Kennedy appeared destined to be the 37th President of the
United States, until he was shot dead in a Los Angeles hotel.

Sirhan Sirhan was disarmed and arrested at the scene, but was he
the only gunman to fire at Kennedy on that fateful night?

THE EVENTS

On March 16, 1968—less than five years after his elder brother, former president John F. Kennedy, had been assassinated in Dallas—Robert F. Kennedy announced his intention to make his own run for president. The 42-year-old had served as his brother's attorney general, and was a U.S. senator for the state of New York when he decided to challenge the sitting President Lyndon Baines Johnson.

The younger Kennedy had watched Johnson preside over the United States' growing involvement in the Vietnam War and the country's simmering racial tensions, which would explode after the assassination of Dr. Martin Luther King, Junior.

For many, Kennedy appeared to offer a divided nation a return to the idealism of his brother's administration, and sensing the growing mood of discontent Johnson withdrew from the race. After winning the Indiana and Nebraska primaries in the spring of 1968, Kennedy secured the Democratic nomination by adding two more victories in California and South Dakota on June 4.

A visibly excited Kennedy celebrated by addressing a ballroom full of his supporters at the Ambassador

Busboy Juan Romero cradles the body of Senator Robert F. Kennedy seconds after he had been fatally shot in 1968.

Sirhan Sirhan posing for police photographs after his arrest for shooting Kennedy in June 1968.

Hotel in Los Angeles. Just after midnight he left the stage with his wife Ethel and walked into the large kitchen accompanied by a group of newspaper reporters, all keen to speak to him, and supporters.

A 22-year-old Palestinian, with Jordanian citizenship, Sirhan Sirhan was hiding next to an ice machine. When he saw Kennedy, he stepped forward and fired three shots from a revolver. However, Kennedy was shot in his head, armpit, chest, and neck. Kennedy collapsed onto the kitchen floor as Sirhan continued to fire into the crowd, before one of Kennedy's bodyguards, William Barry, snatched the gun away. "I knew immediately it was a .22, a small caliber, so I hoped it wouldn't be so bad, but then I saw the hole in the senator's head, and I knew," Barry later recalled.

Busboy Juan Romero, who had only just shaken Kennedy's hand, now cradled his head as the senator asked, "Is everybody okay?" Romero said "Yes," before Kennedy added, "Everything's going to be okay." Kennedy was rushed to the Hospital of the Good Samaritan where he underwent brain surgery to remove the bullet fragments, but it wasn't enough, and at 1:44 a.m. on June 6, he was declared dead.

THE THEORIES

Sirhan had shot Kennedy in front of over 30 witnesses and was immediately arrested at the scene. He confessed his guilt in an interview with Los Angeles police on June 9, declaring he wanted to punish the senator for his public support for the state of Israel.

On April 17, 1969, Sirhan was convicted of Kennedy's murder and sentenced to the death penalty six days later, but in 1972 this was commuted to life in prison. He has spent the last 53 years behind bars, and currently resides at the Richard J. Donovan Correctional Facility in San Diego.

The mystery surrounding Kennedy's assassination has always been about whether Sirhan acted alone or had accomplices on the night. The theory there was a second gunman has long been a matter of debate because of where the bullets hit. The Los Angeles coroner Thomas Noguchi stated that the fatal shot behind Kennedy's right ear was fired from just an inch away. However, witnesses placed Sirhan around 18 inches (45 cm) away when he fired his shots.

Several experts have said that a bullet lodged in Kennedy, and bullets found in other people who had been in the kitchen, were not from the gun fired by Sirhan, with an internal police document including the comment that the Kennedy bullet was not fired from Sirhan's revolver.

Polish journalist Stanisław Pruszyński unearthed the only known recording of the shooting, and had passed it to the audio engineer Philip van Praag, whose analysis found 13 shots were fired that night. However, Sirhan's gun only contained eight bullets, and he fired all of them and wasn't able to reload, prompting the question, where did the extra shots come from?

"The conclusion is inescapable," van Praag wrote in 2011, "that there was a second gun fired by a second shooter during the shooting that resulted in the death of Senator Robert F. Kennedy, and that the five shots from the second gun were fired in a direction opposite the direction in which Sirhan fired."

However, over the last half a century, the identity of this presumed second gunman has remained elusive.

In 1968 a Kennedy campaign worker, Sandra Serrano, claimed she saw a woman in a polka-dot dress running through the hotel shouting, "We shot him, we shot him!" But in police files released in 1988, it stated Serrano withdrew her statement two weeks later and admitted "the whole thing was a lie." However, she did defend herself by saying she had been forced to recant her original statement: "There was a lot of badgering going on. I was just 20 years old, and I became unglued...I said what they wanted me to say."

THE MURDER OF SUZANNE TAMIM

LOCATION: . . . . .DUBAI

SUSPECTS: . . . . .MOUSTAFA & AL SUKKARI

VICTIMS: . . . . .SUZANNE TAMIM

DATE: . . . . .JULY 28, 2008

One of the Arab world's leading popstars was found dead, with multiple stab wounds in her face and neck, at her luxury apartment in Dubai.

She had endured a chaotic private life across four countries before her untimely death, but who wielded the knife that fateful night?

THE EVENTS

After winning the top prize on the star-maker show *Studio El Fan* in 1996, Suzanne Tamim emerged as one of the biggest popstars in the Arab world. The strikingly beautiful Lebanese singer was feted for her melodic voice and ability to sing both Arabic and classic pop songs. She became equally famous for her private life, and by the time of her death at the age of 30, had already had two failed marriages, first to university classmate Ali Mouzannar, then to music producer Adel Matouk.

During her marriage to Matouk he was also her music manager, but Tamim soon found him to be too possessive and controlling. In 2003 it was reported when Tamim had traveled to the United States to play a series of concerts, Matouk sought a civil court order requiring her to return home to Lebanon, and sued her for violating Lebanese civil law by leaving home without his permission. Three years later, Matouk accused Tamim of stealing $350,000 from him, and had her arrested while working in Cairo. She was cleared of the charges.

Tamim was determined to escape from Matouk and forge a new life for herself in Egypt. There she was introduced to Hisham Talaat Moustafa, one of the country's most powerful and richest men. The billionaire property mogul, who was also a high-ranking government official as a member of the ruling National Democratic Party's Supreme Policies Council, became enamored with Tamim and began to act as a patron, helping her establish herself in Egypt. It is believed they also entered into a romantic relationship, but this has never been fully established.

Tamim was one of the Arab world's biggest popstars in the late 1990s.

Left to right: Mohsen al Sukkari and Hisham Moustafa during a court hearing.

"She saw in him the person who could protect her and the person who could remove her from her problems, I think that's why she got involved with Talaat," Joe Raad, Tamim's friend and stylist, told ABC News in 2008.

Once again, however, Tamim found herself falling under the control of a jealous and manipulative man. Her family noticed she was dressing more conservatively in her pop videos and began to pray more, even taking two trips to Mecca.

"She was full of fear and anxiety," Raad added. "She had a feeling that something was going to happen to her. She would always tell me 'I'm afraid.' Through her manner I could tell that Moustafa was not just a jealous man, but more than that, possessive, but extremely generous."

Tamim would leave Cairo for London, where she met Riyadh Al-Azzawi, a British-Iraqi kickboxing champion. The pair soon married, and together purchased a luxury apartment in the Rimal Tower, in Dubai. Tamim was there on her own on the evening of July 28, 2008, when she opened her apartment door and was killed instantly by an assailant who stabbed her multiple times, and is also reported to have slit her throat.

THE THEORIES

Within five hours of her death, Dubai police arrested and charged former Egyptian police officer Mohsen Al Sukkari. A shoe print found in the apartment took investigators to the Dubai store where the shoe had been purchased, which led them to Al Sukkari. He had been filmed on the complex's CCTV system, and incriminating DNA was found on his clothes. Al Sukkari quickly implicated Hisham Talaat Moustafa, claiming the billionaire had paid him $2 million to kill Tamim.

The pair went on trial in 2009 in Cairo, where the court listened to transcripts of recorded telephone conversations between the two men. "The best solution is for her to be thrown from the balcony, like what happened with Ashraf Marwan in London," Moustafa was heard saying, referring to the case of an Egyptian billionaire who died after falling from a balcony in 2007. "The agreed-upon amount is ready. She is in London...deal with it." Al Sukkari replied, "The place for it to be carried out has moved to Dubai... the matter needs careful preparation...she has many people around her."

In May 2009 Al Sukkari and Moustafa were both found guilty of being involved in Tamim's murder and sentenced to death, but 10 months later the court threw out the convictions. After a retrial, Moustafa was sentenced to 15 years, and Al Sukkari to life in prison.

The motive appeared to be revenge by Moustafa, who reportedly wanted to make Tamim his wife. "Suzanne told me that he had phoned her and said that if she left me and went to marry him he would pay her $50 million. He then said that if she refused he would then kill her," her third husband Al-Alazzawi told *The Sunday Times* in 2008. Moustafa was released from prison on health grounds with a presidential pardon in 2017; in 2020 Al Sukkari was also released and granted a pardon by President Abdel Fattah el-Sisi.

3

UNSOLVED MURDERS

We have a natural desire for
answers, but you won't find many
of them here, as we look at some
of the most compelling cases of
unsolved murders, including the
British TV presenter Jill Dando,
gunned down outside her house,
the mutilated body of Elizabeth
Short, known as the Black Dahlia,
found in Los Angeles, and "God's
Banker" Roberto Calvi, who was
discovered hanging beneath a
London bridge.

THE
WANDA BEACH
MURDERS

LOCATION: ....SYDNEY, AUSTRALIA

VICTIMS: 2

DATE: ....JANUARY 11, 1965

The discovery of two 15-year-old girls lying dead on a Sydney beach sparked the biggest police investigation in Australian history.

They had both been stabbed and sexually assaulted on sand dunes within sight of a surf club, but at first the police had few clues.

Who murdered Marianne and Christine on Wanda Beach?

THE EVENTS

During their school summer holidays in 1965, two 15-year-old girls, Marianne Schmidt and Christine Sharrock, set off on what they hoped would be a day of fun and adventure at a local beach. The pair, from the Sydney suburb of West Ryde, took the train south to Cronulla beach, but because Marianne's mother was not well, Marianne was forced to take her four younger siblings, Norbert, Wolfgang, Peter, and Trixie.

The group arrived at Cronulla at around 11:00 a.m., and were disappointed to be greeted by overcast skies and windy conditions, which had closed the beach. Nonetheless, Marianne and Christine were determined to enjoy their day, and headed south on the beach, where they found an area of rocks that afforded them some protection from the wind. At one point, Christine disappeared for an unexplained short spell, and on her return, the group decided to head even further south before settling down behind a sand dune near the Wanda Surf Club.

Police and civilian volunteers comb the beach for clues.

The younger children were now getting tired, but Marianne and Christine told them they were going to collect their bags from the area of the beach they had been at earlier, and left them to listen to a radio while they were gone. When the girls set off in the wrong direction, Peter shouted at them, but they shrugged, laughed, and continued on their way. At around 5:00 p.m., with the wind still blowing sand in their faces, the younger children decided to go looking for the two girls, and though they found their bags, there was no sign of the girls, so the children decided to head home.

Bodies in the sand

On their return to West Ryde, Christine's grandmother alerted the police when the children told her the girls had left them on their own and disappeared. The following afternoon, 17-year-old Peter Smith was walking along Wanda Beach with his three young nephews when he spotted what he first thought was a mannequin in the sand, before realizing it was the body of a young girl.

When the police arrived, they quickly discovered there were two bodies there in the sand. Marianne was on her side with her swimsuit cut open; Christine was lying facedown. The police thought that the drag marks in the sand indicated the victims had been placed next to each other after being killed. It appeared Marianne had been murdered first, then Christine caught as she tried to escape, before she was killed too, and dragged back to where they were both found.

The autopsies found the two girls had been victims of a horrific and violent sexual attack. Marianne had been stabbed many times and had had her throat cut so severely she was almost decapitated. Christine had been stabbed 14 times and her skull had been fractured with a blow to the back of her head. There was evidence the murderer had attempted to rape the girls, with semen being found on both of them.

The police found a knife in the sand, but were unable to take fingerprints from it, and tire tracks in a nearby parking lot; but their investigations drew a blank.

THE THEORIES

The first lead came from Marianne's eight-year-old brother, Wolfgang, who said he had seen a teenage boy crab-hunting with a knife or spear. The teenager was seen speaking to both Marianne and Christine that day, but police never tracked him down, and to this day he remains unidentified.

A Wanda Beach lifeguard told police in the days before the murders a man had been sexually harassing girls on the beach, and he had to physically remove him, but once again this man was never identified.

One suspect police named was Christopher Wilder, "The Beauty Queen Killer," who abducted 12 women, killing at least eight of them, during a six-week spell in the United States in 1984. Wilder was from Sydney, and had emigrated to the United States aged 24 in 1969, and, crucially, was living in the city at the time the two girls were murdered. Police files from the time have shown he was an official suspect, who had been brought to their attention by his own wife in 1968, but before they had followed up her tip, he had moved to the United States.

"In my mind, it would have to be Christopher Wilder because there are so many signs to this guy that point to his sexual deviancy, his propensity for violence and [he] was around in Sydney at the time, hung around the beaches," retired Detective Inspector Ian Waterson said in 2018. After his horrific killing spree in 1984, Wilder had shot himself in the heart to avoid capture by the police.

In 1969 pedophile Derek Percy was jailed for killing 12-year-old Yvonne Tuohy on a beach in Victoria. Police believe Percy could also have been responsible for the Wanda Beach murders, as he was in the area on the day and had a resemblance to the teenage crab-catcher. When asked about Christine and Marianne's murders, he replied, "I could have done it, but I can't remember." He died in prison in 2013 without revealing anything more.

THE
DOORSTEP
KILLER

LOCATION: ....LONDON, UK

VICTIM: ....JILL DANDO

DATE: ....APRIL 26, 1999

On a quiet London street, in the light of day, a popular television presenter was ruthlessly killed on her doorstep with a single shot to the head. No one heard the gunfire, just a brief scream as she was pushed to the ground, where she then lay, bleeding to death, as her killer walked calmly away.

The police launched the biggest murder inquiry since the Yorkshire Ripper, nearly 20 years before, as they took 2,400 statements and interviewed around 2,000 potential suspects, while wrestling with the question: Who would want to kill Jill Dando?

THE EVENTS

On a bright spring morning in 1999, BBC Television presenter Jill Dando left her fiancé Alan Farthing's house in the west London suburb of Chiswick to make the short journey by car to her house in Fulham, in southwest London. The 37-year-old was due to marry Farthing in September that year, and was now living with him most of the time. She had put her own house up for sale, and returned to it only intermittently.

On arrival at the smart terraced house on Gowan Avenue, at 11:30 a.m., Dando was reaching to put her keys in the door lock when she was suddenly grabbed from behind with force, which would leave a bruise on her arm. The assailant pushed her down on her doorstep, and with her face touching the ground, killed her with one shot to her left temple. The single bullet entered her head above her ear, and left on the right side of her head, before lodging low down in the front door.

Dando's neighbor Richard Hughes would recall how she made a brief and startled sound: "It was a very distinctive scream. She sounded quite surprised." He went to investigate and found her lying on her doorstep in a pool of blood. Hughes would later realize he had seen the killer pass by his window immediately afterward, describing him as a white male, around 40 years old, about 6 feet (1.8 meters) tall, clean shaven with dark hair, and wearing a suit. Hughes thought the assailant was holding a cell phone in his

After Jill Dando was shot by an unknown gunman in southwest London, flowers were laid on her doorstep.

The victim's well-attended funeral procession to her final resting place at a cemetery in Weston-super-Mare in May 1999.

hand, but would come to accept it was probably the gun used in the murder. Hughes would later suggest the time between hearing Dando close the door of her BMW convertible and the sound of the front gate being closed by her fleeing murderer was a mere 30 seconds.

After shooting Dando, the killer had turned left to walk along Gowan Avenue, walking quickly at first, then breaking into a run and disappearing. Dando lay there on her doorstep, still clutching her keys and with her handbag over her shoulder, as her cell rang several times. Neighbors on Gowan Avenue phoned an ambulance, but Dando was declared dead on arrival at Charing Cross Hospital, just after 1:00 p.m.

The senseless nature of Dando's death greatly affected the British public, becoming a national moment of deep sorrow, with both the Queen and Prime Minister Tony Blair paying her warm tributes.

Dando was a presenter
on the long-running BBC
show Crimewatch, which
sought to solve crimes.

BACKGROUND

At the time of her death, Jill Dando was one of the UK's most respected and
beloved television presenters. She was due to host the *BBC Six O'Clock News*
the night after her murder, and just two weeks later The British Academy of
Film, Television, and Arts awards with Michael Parkinson at the Grosvenor
House Hotel in London.

Born in Weston-super-Mare, in the west of England, in November 1961, Dando
started her career at weekly newspaper the *Weston Mercury* before progressing
through the ranks at the BBC, first with several local roles in her native
Southwest before becoming one of the corporation's biggest names.

She was best known as a newsreader, and for presenting *Crimewatch* and
the long-running travel program *Holiday* that allowed her to travel across
the world.

THE THEORIES

In the days that followed the murder, after the shock at Dando's death there was a strong sense of bewilderment as to why anyone would want to kill her. There was no robbery, nothing was taken; there was no sexual assault or attempted rape; this was a straightforward assassination.

In May 2000, 13 months after Dando's death, the police thought they had their answer when they arrested and charged local man Barry George. He fitted the role of an obsessed fan, who lived just 500 yards (450 meters) from Dando's home, and had previous convictions for attempted rape and indecent assault. He also had some experience with guns after his time as a member of the Territorial Army in the early 1980s, and on searching his apartment police found photos of thousands of women, as well as articles on Dando. The final piece of the puzzle appeared to be the discovery of a microscopic particle in the pocket of George's coat that a forensic scientist said could be firearms residue.

In July 2001 George was found guilty and sentenced to life imprisonment at the Old Bailey, but there was always a sense of unease at the conviction. On his third appeal in 2007, once the firearms residue evidence had been discredited, George's conviction was quashed, and he was acquitted after a retrial the following year. With George now in the clear, the strongest theory has long been Dando was killed by a trained Serbian hitman in an act of calculated revenge.

Barry George was found guilty of Dando's murder before his conviction was eventually quashed.

A revenge attack?

Three weeks before her murder, Dando had fronted a charity appeal on behalf of Kosovan refugees who were under attack by the Serbs in the protracted Balkans conflict, and three days before she died, NATO forces, including the UK, had bombed Serbian state television, killing 16 people. The police files contained intelligence Dando's murder was linked to these NATO attacks, which was fueled further by an anonymous phone call placed to the BBC the day after she died that said, "Your Prime Minister Blair murdered, butchered 17 innocent young people...He butchered, we butcher back. The first one you had yesterday. The next one will be [Chief Executive of BBC News] Tony Hall."

The professional nature of Dando's murder, the single shot to the head, the possible use of a silencer, before the killer disappeared in broad daylight, encouraged the belief it was carried out by a hit man.

Dando's position as a *Crimewatch* presenter, a program that actively sought to bring criminals to justice, was an obvious line of enquiry: Could she have been murdered as an act of revenge for helping to send someone to prison? The police took this line of enquiry seriously, ruling out a list of up to 30 people who might harbor some resentment to *Crimewatch*, and even spoke to convicted contract killers serving sentences in prison, but found nothing.

Overall, what most undermined this theory was that Dando, a mere TV presenter, would be the focus of a vengeful attack instead of an actual informant or an individual who had testified against a criminal.

THE
DEATH OF
INNOCENCE

LOCATION: .... BOULDER, COLORADO, USA

VICTIM: .... JONBENÉT RAMSEY

DATE: .... DECEMBER 25, 1996

In the early hours of the morning, police were summoned to a mansion in Boulder by a frantic mother who was saying her six-year-old daughter had been kidnapped and they had been left a ransom note.

It would be seven hours later that her father would discover that, in fact, the body of JonBenét Ramsey was in the basement of her family home. She had been strangled with a garrote and struck on the head.

A missing person case had now become a murder case, but there were very few leads, as suspicion began to swirl around the parents.

Who killed the child beauty pageant queen JonBenét Ramsay?

THE EVENTS

At the foothills of Colorado's Rocky Mountains, in the university town of Boulder, the Ramsey family of John, Patsy, their nine-year-old son Burke and six-year-old daughter JonBenét enjoyed Christmas Day in 1996, opening presents in the morning before having lunch at a friend's house.

They returned to their Tudor mansion at around 10:00 p.m. that night, before heading to bed and setting an early alarm for the next morning as they were taking a flight to Michigan for a short break at their holiday cottage. At around 5:50 a.m., Patsy woke first and descended the spiral staircase, where at the bottom step she found three pieces of paper neatly lined up together.

To her horror, she discovered that her daughter JonBenét had seemingly been kidnapped, and this was a ransom note demanding money for her return:

Mr. Ramsey, Listen carefully! We are a group of individuals that represent a small foreign faction. We do respect your bussiness [sic] but not the country that it serves. At this time we have your daughter in our posession [sic]. She is safe and unharmed and if you want her to see 1997, you must follow our instructions to the letter. You will withdraw $118,000.00 from your account. $100,000 will be in $100 bills and the remaining $18,000 in $20 bills...Any deviation of my instructions will result in the immediate execution of your daughter.

The Tudor mansion in Boulder, Colorado, where JonBenét Ramsay was found murdered in the basement.

"I dashed back upstairs, pushed open the door to JonBenét's bedroom, and screamed for John," Patsy recalled. Despite the ransom note telling them not to call for any help, they phoned 911 and two police officers were at the house within three minutes. They made a cursory search of the house without finding anything, then radioed for further support and a forensics team. Meanwhile, the Ramseys had called several local friends to join them at the house.

The problem was only JonBenét's bedroom had been cordoned off to prevent any contamination of evidence, and nothing else in the house. "The police did a terrible, terrible job securing that scene...and if you don't secure the scene, you don't get good evidence," said Diane Dimond, an investigative reporter. "People were streaming through that house. They were in the kitchen, they were in the living room. There were some friends of Patsy's that were helping her wipe up the kitchen. There could've been fingerprints there." Even the ransom note was being passed around and read by friends.

The Ramseys, who were preparing to pay the ransom to the kidnappers, had been told that they would be called between 8:00 a.m. and 10:00 a.m. that morning, but a call never came.

At around 1:00 p.m., by which time most of the police had left the house, the Ramseys were with Detective Linda Arndt, who suggested to John and family friend Fleet White that they might make another search of the house. They first ventured down to the basement—where behind a door they found the body of JonBenét on the floor. Her mouth had been covered with duct tape and there was a cord around her wrists and neck. In a further breach of protocol, John picked up his daughter's body and took it upstairs. It was the understandable reaction of a shocked and grieving parent but should not have been allowed, and further contaminated the crime scene.

Any hopes the child might still be alive were quickly extinguished, and Arndt confirmed she was dead. An autopsy gave the official cause of death as "asphyxia by strangulation associated with craniocerebral trauma." She had been strangled with a garrote made from a nylon cord and the broken handle of a paintbrush, and there was an 8-inch (20-cm) fracture across her skull. There was also evidence of a vaginal injury, with that area of her body having been wiped down with a cloth.

In her brief
life JonBenét
won several
child beauty
pageants.

BACKGROUND

JonBenét was born in Atlanta, Georgia, in 1990 and given the unusual name with its French pronunciation as a tribute to her father John Bennett. The following year, the family moved to Boulder, where the headquarters of her father's Access Graphics computer software firm was located.

Mother Patsy enthusiastically introduced JonBenét to the world of child beauty pageants, where she was crowned Little Miss Colorado, Little Miss Charlevoix, Colorado State All-Star Kids Cover Girl, America's Royale Miss, and National Tiny Miss Beauty. It has often been said the sheer volume of pictures and footage of JonBenét competing in these pageants—with a full face of makeup and striking adult poses—is what inspired so much public fascination with her murder.

THE THEORIES

The theories surrounding JonBenét's death have long centered on whether she was murdered by a member of her family or a stranger who had broken into their house.

The parents immediately became suspects for their daughter's death, simply because there were no signs of forced entry or evidence of an intruder. There was a ransom note of course, but that baffled police because it was so rambling, no one had ever seen one so long. It was also written with a pen that had come from within the house, and on one of Patsy's notepads. In addition, the garrote used to kill JonBenét was made from a broken paintbrush that came from Patsy's art supplies in the house. The amount demanded in the note was also curious: $118,000 is a strange amount, but more importantly, it matched what John had been given as a bonus in the previous year. Who could have known this?

One theory is Patsy had struck JonBenét with enough force to kill her, and then strangled her to cover it up and make it look even more sinister, but she had no history of violence toward her children or anyone. Some suspicion fell on JonBenét's older brother, Burke: Had he killed her by accident? But investigators interviewed him three times and learned nothing to concern them, and in 1998 Boulder police publicly declared he was not involved in any way with her death.

In 2013 it was revealed that back in 1999 a Colorado grand jury indicted the Ramseys, accusing them of "two counts each of child abuse" and said they "did unlawfully, knowingly, recklessly, and feloniously permit a child to be unreasonably placed in a situation that posed a threat of injury to the child's life or health, which resulted in the death of JonBenét Ramsey." But the District Attorney Alex Hunter felt unable to sign the indictment, believing there was not enough credible evidence to prosecute.

In later years, DNA evidence would be unearthed that likely vindicated this decision. By 2008 technology had improved enough to allow DNA to be taken from the legs of JonBenét's pajamas and from inside her underwear drawer. It did not match any of the Ramsey family, and instead belonged to an unknown male. The serving District Attorney Mary Lacy told the Ramseys they had been "completely cleared" by the DNA evidence.

Alternative evidence and suspects

Lou Smit, a Colorado detective who was assigned the case in 1998, never believed there was enough evidence to make the parents suspects. He believed an open window in the basement, left ajar for a Christmas lights cord, which he himself proved a person could go through, was a major clue, as was the discovery of a shoe print of a Hi-Tec sneaker next to JonBenét's body, when none of the family owned a pair of that brand. There was also, he believed, evidence a stun gun had been used on JonBenét's body, which no one in the house owned either.

There were several other suspects, but each time they were investigated they would be cleared. Michael Helgoth owned a pair of Hi-Tec trainers and a stun gun, and had committed suicide not long after JonBenét's murder, but his DNA did not match that found at the scene. Bill McReynolds had known the family after dressing up as Santa Claus for parties at their house for the previous three years, but again his DNA did not match. A homeless man named Gary Oliva, who was a regular at the Ramsey's local church, had told a friend he had killed a little girl, but beyond that there was nothing to place him at the house on the night.

JonBenét is buried in Marietta, Georgia, next to Patsy, who died of ovarian cancer in 2006, and her half-sister Elizabeth, who died in a car crash in 1992.

SLAUGHTER
AT
HINTERKAIFECK
FARM

LOCATION: ..HINTERKAIFECK FARM, GERMANY

VICTIMS: 6

DATE: ....MARCH 31, 1922

When a young girl didn't turn up for school and a mailbox began to overflow, a group of villagers went to investigate what was happening at a farm in southern Germany.

They found four bodies inside a barn, and two further bodies inside the house. All had been struck in the head with a mattock.

Who bludgeoned to death six people at Hinterkaifeck Farm, and why?

THE EVENTS

Hinterkaifeck was an isolated farm in the southern German state of Bavaria. Six people lived there: 63-year-old Andreas Gruber and his 72-year-old wife Cäzilia; their 35-year-old widowed daughter Viktoria Gabriel; her children, seven-year-old Cäzilia and two-year-old Josef; and newly appointed 44-year-old maid Maria Baumgartner. The Grubers were thought to be a relatively well-off family who closely guarded their privacy and made little effort to socialize with other villagers.

Toward the end of 1921, the family's previous maid had quit because she was tired of hearing footsteps coming from the farm's attic, and would later tell police. She had said it was a feeling of being watched that convinced her to leave, and the rest of the family had also heard the noises. Around the same time, Andreas noticed there were footsteps from the nearby woods that led all the way to his house, but strangely they stopped there, and there were none leading back the other way.

Andreas had also found a Munich newspaper near his house, on the edge of the wood, that didn't belong to him or any of his neighbors, and the mailman had no recollection of delivering it to anyone in the local area. To add to Andreas's sense of unease, he had mislaid the only key he had to his house and believed it had been stolen, rather than simply lost.

On March 31, 1922, the new maid, Maria Baumgartner, had arrived at the farm. She was dropped off by her sister, who would be the last person to see her and the Gruber family alive.

Whoever killed the Grubers mysteriously stayed on the farm afterward to feed the animals.

Investigators believe a mattock was used to murder all six people at Hinterkaifeck Farm.

By April 4, locals realized that no one had seen the Grubers for the last four days. The youngest, Cäzilia, had not turned up at school, and the mailman noticed nothing had been collected from the mailbox for several days.

At around 5:00 p.m. on that day, three neighbors, Lorenz Schlittenbauer, Michael Poll, and Jakob Sigl, went to the farm to investigate—and found the battered bodies of Andreas, Cäzilia, Viktoria, and her daughter Cäzilia in the barn. On entering the main house, they soon found the bodies of Maria Baumgartner and Viktoria's son, Josef, who had been murdered in his crib. An autopsy revealed they had all been killed with a blunt instrument, possibly a hammer-like mattock that had delivered several blows to their heads, which had cracked their skulls and damaged their faces.

THE THEORIES

The police had few clues to go on, even after scouring the local area and taking over a hundred statements, but they were able to establish the murders had taken place on the evening of March 31 and that, rather strangely, the perpetrator had then stayed at the house for several nights, eating food from the kitchen and feeding the family's cattle.

However, over time, the criminal inspector Georg Reingruber began to collate a list of suspects. The original suspect was Josef Bartl, who had recently escaped from a mental asylum 45 miles (70 km) from the farm. Reingruber sought to link Bartl to the crime, as he heard a story that Bartl had been asking for a place to hide and offered a stranger a 100-mark note stained with blood. But forensic investigations could not link the money to the farm. Bartl himself was never found, and there was never any evidence he had been at the farm, or even knew it existed. The trail went cold.

The strongest suspect

The most persistent suspect has been the man who discovered the bodies:
Lorenz Schlittenbauer. He knew the farm well, lived nearby, and spoke
with all the residents there. There was also a simmering tension between
Schlittenbauer and Andreas after Schlittenbauer had enjoyed a romantic
relationship with his daughter Viktoria. The pair had wanted to marry, but
Andreas refused to allow it. When Schlittenbauer learned about Andreas's
incestuous relationship with Viktoria he reported it to the police. It had been
rumored Schlittenbauer was the father of Viktoria's son, Josef. He initially
denied it, but would later call him "my boy." There was further speculation he
didn't provide the child with enough financial support.

Above all, it was Schlittenbauer's behavior at the crime scene that most
raised suspicions. On discovering the bodies, he strangely started to move
items around in the barn, began cleaning, and fed the animals, to such an
extent that it alarmed Jakob Sigl and Michael Poll. "Poll and I immediately
told Schlittenbauer when we found the bodies that he should be careful to
leave things as they are, but he replied he had to see things for himself," Sigl
told the police. "He then told me to feed the cattle, but I told him that we
were going home and reporting to the police...He was very busy, he went
straight to the cellar to fetch milk and feed the pigs. It was very striking
Schlittenbauer changed everything that could have been changed and knew
exactly where everything in the house was."

Schlittenbauer always strenuously denied any involvement, and even
received damages for slander from another villager who had suggested he
had played some role in the murders. He was never arrested, and police said
in their final report they found nothing to implicate him.

THE BLACK DAHLIA

LOCATION: ....LOS ANGELES, USA

VICTIM: ....ELIZABETH SHORT

DATE: ....JANUARY 15, 1947

The pallid white body of Elizabeth Short, who would become forever known as the Black Dahlia, was discovered cut into two parts and drained of blood on the empty lot of a Los Angeles street.

The police were at a loss to understand who was responsible for such a heinous crime, and in time would wade through 150 suspects and more than 500 false confessions in their search for the truth.

One of the most famous crimes to capture the world's attention: Who was the Black Dahlia, and why was she murdered?

THE EVENTS

On a January morning in 1947, Betty Bersinger was taking her three-year-old daughter Anne to a shoe repair store in the Leimert Park area of Los Angeles when she noticed something strange on a patch of waste ground. At first, she thought it was a discarded mannequin, but as she got closer she realized—to her horror—it was the mutilated body of a young woman.

"I glanced to my right, and saw this very dead and white body, my goodness, it was so white," Bersinger has recalled. "It didn't look like anything more than perhaps an artificial model. It was so white and separated in the middle."

The police discovered the body was that of 20-year-old Elizabeth Short, who had been cut gruesomely in two parts from the waist. The body had also been carefully arranged by the killer; on her top half, Short's hands were placed over her head, with her elbows bent, and her mouth had been slit at both sides. Her legs had been left spread apart, and on several parts of her body chunks of flesh had been removed.

The dismembered body of Elizabeth Short was found on an empty lot in Los Angeles.

Strangely, there was almost no blood at the scene. The body appeared clean, as though it had been scrubbed and drained of any blood or fluids. Short would later be identified by her fingerprints.

The horrific state of the body, and being found not far from Hollywood, gave the case a macabre sense of glamor and intrigue, fueling huge interest across the country, particularly when the local Los Angeles newspapers began to refer to Short as the "Black Dahlia." The origins of this name are disputed. It is thought Short might have been given it when she was still alive by staff at a drugstore in Long Beach who were inspired by the 1946 movie *The Blue Dahlia*, and adapted it for her because of her black hair and habit of wearing black clothes.

Six days after the murder, the city editor of the *Los Angeles Examiner* James Richardson received an anonymous phone call from a man who claimed to be the killer and said he would be sending him some of Short's belongings. Just three days later, the U.S. Postal Service intercepted a package addressed

Police closely inspect Short's handbag after the killer led them to it days after her death.

Short had aspirations to be an actress in Hollywood, but was murdered before they could be realized.

BACKGROUND

Elizabeth Short was born in July 1924 in Boston, Massachusetts, before being raised in the suburb of Medford by her parents Cleo and Phoebe. When she was six years old her father disappeared, presumed to have committed suicide when his car was found abandoned next to the Charles River in Boston. His body was never found.

Short's mother struggled to bring up a family of five young daughters on her own, until she received a letter in 1942 from her husband announcing he was still alive and living in Vallejo, California. Now aged 18, Short moved to the west coast to live with her father, but it was not a success; the pair constantly argued, she moved out, and in September 1943 Short was arrested for underage drinking in Santa Barbara.

Short made her final move in July 1946 when she relocated to Los Angeles, where she worked as a waitress, with aspirations to become an actress, and lived just off Hollywood Boulevard.

George Hodel was a suspect for Short's murder, who in recent years has been implicated further by his son Steve.

to the *Examiner*. Inside was a message consisting of large cut-out newspaper letters pasted together on a sheet of paper that read, "Here is Dahlia's belongings. Letter to follow," which was accompanied by photographs of Elizabeth Short, her birth certificate, business cards, and an address book with the name Mark Hansen on the cover.

The police were desperately hoping the package and Short's possessions would feature the killer's fingerprints, but they had all been doused in a strong-smelling gasoline to prevent that. However, the FBI still managed to find some, but they were not of great quality and could not be matched.

On the same day the *Examiner* received this package, a handbag and a single shoe belonging to Short were found on top of a garbage can not far from where her body had been discovered, but once again they had been smothered in gasoline and no fingerprints could be recovered.

THE THEORIES

One of the last people to see Short was Robert "Red" Manley, who had spent some time with her in San Diego before returning to Los Angeles and dropping her off at the Biltmore Hotel in the downtown area of the city. He was an obvious suspect, but there was no evidence linking him to her death, and he was cleared after passing several polygraph tests.

The owner of the address book in the package, Mark Hansen, was another suspect, especially as the nightclub owner was known to Short, and friends say he made sexual advances on her, but he too was cleared. Hansen's address book contained several useful early leads, but ultimately they came to nothing.

The medical connection

The manner in which Short's body had been cut in half suggested a surgeon or an individual with medical experience must have been involved, prompting the police to ask the University of Southern California Medical School to provide a complete list of their students, but even in possession of this they could find nothing, and their enquires went nowhere.

In recent years, the former LA detective Steve Hodel has sought to implicate his deceased father George Hodel, due to his medical degree and some evidence he had formed a relationship with Short in 1946. It came to light in 2003 there was a "George Hodel–Black Dahlia" file hidden in a vault in the LA County District Attorney's office, which revealed that Hodel had been a suspect for Short's murder. The police had even managed to place a recording device at his Hollywood house that caught "H" saying, "Suppose I did kill the Black Dahlia. They can't prove it now. They can't talk to my secretary anymore because she's dead."

Hodel had also been a suspect in the death of his secretary Ruth Spaulding in 1945, and Louise Springer in 1949, but along with Short, he was never charged with their murders. In 1950 he fled to the Philippines, where he lived until 1990, before returning to the United States, where he died in 1999.

THE DISAPPEARANCE

OF

LORD LUCAN

LOCATION: .... LONDON, ENGLAND, UK

SUSPECT: .... LORD LUCAN

VICTIM: .... SANDRA RIVETT

DATE: .... NOVEMBER 7, 1974

When police arrived at an expensive Belgravia townhouse they found a heavily bloodstained carpet, a lead pipe smeared with blood, and the body of Sandra Rivett stuffed inside a mail sack.

Hours earlier an assailant, believed to be Lord Lucan, had killed his family's nanny and attacked his estranged wife Veronica before disappearing, never to be seen again.

For nearly 50 years the question has been asked: What happened to Lord Lucan?

THE EVENTS

In May 1974, 29-year-old Sandra Rivett began working for Lady Veronica Lucan, the wife of Lord Lucan, as a nanny to the couple's three young children, Frances, George, and Camilla. The family lived at 46 Lower Belgrave Street in central London, but Lord Lucan had moved out 18 months earlier and had since been embroiled in a bitter divorce and custody battle with Lady Lucan.

On the evening of November 7 that year, Rivett had cancelled a night out with her boyfriend John Hankins to work for the family, and by around 9:00 p.m. had put the two youngest children to bed. Soon after, Rivett asked Lady Lucan if she wanted a cup of tea, before descending the stairs to the basement kitchen to make it. Before she could turn on the light at the bottom of the stairs, an assailant killed her by striking her over the head with a lead pipe, before swiftly putting her bloodied and lifeless body into a canvas mail sack.

Wondering what had happened to the cup of tea Rivett was making, Lady Lucan called to her from the top of the stairs, before she, too, was attacked. She screamed, but was told by her attacker to "Shut up!", which is when she realized it was her husband's voice.

Lord Lucan and his wife Lady Lucan were separated at the time of his disappearance.

Lord Lucan pictured working
on the engine of his
powerboat in 1963.

BACKGROUND

Known as "Lucky" by his friends, Richard John Bingham was a British peer, the
7th Earl of Lucan, most commonly known as Lord Lucan. Born into aristocracy
in 1934, he was the son of George Bingham, the 6th Earl of Lucan, and attended
Eton College. He had spells as a merchant banker, but was more famous for his
skills as a successful gambler at London's leading casinos.

Lucan had been seen as the archetypal suave and stylish English gentleman,
who *The New York Times* once described like a James Bond figure, as "a dashing
aristocrat, known for his prowess at backgammon and bridge, and his fondness
for vodka martinis, powerboats, and Aston Martin cars."

In 1963 he married Veronica Duncan, and the pair would have three children
before they separated in 1972.

He grabbed her by the throat and threw her to the carpeted floor, only letting go of her when she squeezed his testicles.

When Lady Lucan demanded to know what had happened to Rivett, Lucan admitted he had killed her. A strange normality broke out in the house; Lucan ushered his eldest daughter back to bed and went to the house's main bedroom. He asked for some painkillers, and when he disappeared into the bathroom to find them, Lady Lucan took this as her opportunity to escape. At this moment, she still had the composure to realize Lucan had come to the house to kill her and had murdered Rivett by mistake thinking it was her. She believed he could quickly return to his original plan at any point.

Terrified and covered in blood, she ran from the house and into the nearby Plumber's Arms pub screaming, "Help me, help me! I have just escaped from a murder. He's in my house. He's murdered the nanny." The pub's head barman Derrick Whitehouse has recalled how Lady Lucan staggered in and said, "I think my neck has been broken. He tried to strangle me." He said she was in "just a delirious state" and had "various head wounds" that were "quite severe."

The last traces

It is known Lucan went first to his friend Madelaine Florman's house at nearby Chester Square at around 10:00 p.m. He knocked at the door, but because of the time of night, she ignored it. She later found bloodstains on her doorstep. Lucan is believed to have then phoned his mother, to tell her something dreadful had happened and to ask her to collect his children from their home.

When police searched Lucan's apartment on nearby Elizabeth Street they found his wallet, money, car keys, his Mercedes parked outside, his driver's license, and his passport. They felt he could not have gone very far.

He had, in fact, made it just over 45 miles (70 km) south to the town of Uckfield, in East Sussex, to pay a visit to his friends Ian and Susan Maxwell-Scott at around midnight, and while there wrote two letters to his brother-in-law Bill Shand Kydd and sent them to his London address. Lucan wrote about "the most ghastly circumstances" and gave an account about how he had interrupted a fight at Lower Belgrave Street between Lady Lucan and a strange man. According to Lucan, his estranged wife accused him of hiring

Divers search Newhaven harbor for signs of the missing murderer, to no avail.

this man to attack her. "The circumstantial evidence against me is strong in that V will say it was all my doing," he added. "I will lie doggo for a bit."

On the following day, the Ford Corsair car Lucan had used to stage his getaway was found in the coastal town of Newhaven, with bloodstains detected around the seats, and a lead pipe matching the murder weapon in the trunk. An inquest would later determine Lucan had murdered Rivett, but until this day he has never been seen again.

THE THEORIES

Before her death in 2017, Lady Lucan gave a television interview in which she said it was her firm belief her husband had boarded a ferry to France before jumping into the English Channel. "[He did it] in the way of the propellers so that his remains wouldn't be found, I think quite brave."

Roy Ranson, the detective leading the investigation, initially said he also believed Lucan had "done the honorable thing" and "fallen on his sword," a view that was shared by many of his friends.

A good friend and fellow gambler at the Clermont Club, James Wilson, told the *Telegraph* in 2015 it was his understanding Lucan had weighed himself down with large stones before jumping off a boat and drowning in Newhaven harbor. "I believe that when he realized he had killed the nanny, the remorse, guilt, and panic lead him to commit suicide. John Lucan was a gambler. He gambled on successfully killing his wife and being able to hide her body and get away with murder. But when it went terribly wrong he must have realized he only had two options open to him: hand himself in or kill himself. Having lost the gamble, he chose the latter."

Shirley Robey, a former assistant to the casino and wild park owner John Aspinall, who was close friends with Lucan, said she had heard her boss suggesting that Lucan had fled overseas. "I knew he was hiding, I knew he was in Africa, I knew we were hushing it up," she said in 2012. "I knew he'd fallen out with his wife and I knew it was a major secret, but for whatever reason I didn't appreciate there had been a murder until some years later."

Another old gambling friend, Philippe Marcq, suggested Lucan killed himself before being fed to a pack of tigers at Howletts, the wildlife park outside Canterbury, in Kent, owned by Aspinall. When police visited Howletts, Aspinall is said to have responded: "My tigers are only fed the choicest cuts—do you really think they're going to eat stringy old Lucky [Lucan]?"

In the last 47 years, Lucan's disappearance has gripped the public's imagination, and there have been more than 70 sightings of him across the world, including in Australia, France, Colombia, Gabon, New Zealand, and South Africa. In 2003 former Scotland Yard detective Duncan McLaughlin claimed Lucan had lived in Goa, India, before dying in 1996. A photograph was produced that showed a man who resembled him with a long gray beard. It was soon revealed the man was actually a banjo player from Merseyside called Barry Halpin, who was also known as Jungle Barry.

In February 2016 Lucan was declared officially dead when a presumption of death certificate was issued to his son George.

THE
DEATH OF
GOD'S BANKER

LOCATION:.............................LONDON, UK

VICTIM:...........................ROBERTO CALVI

DATE:.............................JUNE 18, 1982

On a summer's morning, a man's body was discovered hanging underneath Blackfriars Bridge, on the river Thames in London.

This was no ordinary victim—this was Roberto Calvi, known as "God's Banker" for his links to the Vatican, whose death launched a massive investigation that continues still today.

Did Calvi commit suicide, or did dark forces murder him?

THE EVENTS

In the summer of 1982, the Italian bank chairman Roberto Calvi found himself at the heart of a complex and dangerous international fraud scandal. At the start of the 1970s, Calvi became the general manager of Italy's second largest bank, Banco Ambrosiano, before being promoted to chairman in 1975, which could have been seen as reward for securing the Vatican as a client. Toward the end of the decade, the Vatican, with its vast reserves of wealth, had become one of the largest shareholders in Banco Ambrosiano, giving Calvi a position of immense power and influence in Italy.

However, in 1978 the Bank of Italy had established that Banco Ambrosiano, under Calvi's leadership, had illegally exported several billions of lire. In 1981 Calvi was found guilty of illegally transferring this money out of the country, in violation of Italian currency laws, and was handed a four-year suspended prison sentence and a fine of $19.8 million. Yet Calvi was allowed to remain free after he lodged an appeal against this sentence, though he was now in a severely distressed state, and claimed he had attempted to commit suicide during a short stay in prison.

Blackfriars Bridge stands in the shadow of St. Paul's Cathedral, in the center of London.

Damage limitation

Out on bail and fearful for his life, on June 5, 1982, Calvi felt compelled to write a personal letter to Pope John II warning him Banco Ambrosiano was on the brink of collapse and could "provoke a catastrophe of unimaginable proportions in which the Church will suffer the gravest damage."

Five days later, Calvi disappeared under the cover of night when he fled Italy on a speedboat from the port of Trieste and arrived in Yugoslavia on a false passport. He initially hid away in a modest hotel in Klagenfurt, Austria, before moving on to Bregenz, near the border with Germany. On the evening of June 14, Calvi drove to Innsbruck, where he took a private jet to London before checking in to a rundown room at the Chelsea Cloisters lodgings in southwest London. He was accompanied everywhere by an attaché case said to contain secrets that could harm his well-known clients.

Calvi was desperately trying to broker a deal to save Banco Ambrosiano, but learned on June 17 its directors had dismissed him and suspended the bank's trading on the stock exchange when they had discovered they were $1.4 billion in debt.

Calvi's secretary, Graziella Corrocher, consumed with shame and guilt, committed suicide by throwing herself out of a fifth-floor window at the bank's Milan headquarters after leaving a note highly critical of Calvi.

At around 7:30 a.m. on June 18, a mail worker hurried to work along the Thames path and was shocked to see a man's body hanging from underneath Blackfriars Bridge. It was low tide and so the body could be seen dangling from scaffolding 15 feet (5 meters) from the wall on the north side of the bridge. The man was identified as Calvi, who was wearing a black suit and coat, with the pockets crammed full of bricks to weigh him down. He was also in possession of cash worth around $15,000, in three different currencies.

Calvi found himself
at the center of a
complex and deadly
financial scandal.

BACKGROUND

Roberto Calvi was born in 1920 into a relatively wealthy family in Milan,
headed by his father who was the manager of Banca Commerciale Italiana.
Instead of going to university, Calvi joined the army at the start of World
War II, and served on the Russian front, where he was given awards by both his
own country and the Nazis. On his return, Calvi joined his father's bank, and
worked at a branch in Lecce, in southern Italy, before moving to Catholic Banca
Ambrosiano, in his native Milan, in 1946.

Calvi was described as a workaholic, which would help his rise, and he would
earn a position as the personal assistant to the bank's president, Carlo Canesi.
In 1952 Calvi married Clara Cancelli, and over the next seven years they had
two children, Carlo and Anna.

THE THEORIES

On July 23, 1982, an inquest ruled Calvi's death was suicide, but the following year this was overturned in a second inquest that produced an open verdict. The Calvi family were convinced he had been murdered, and in 1991 commissioned the private investigation company Kroll Associates to prove it.

Over the course of a two-year investigation, which included the work of forensic scientists, Kroll concluded Calvi could not have hung himself. There was no paint, rust, or brick dust found on his fingers, clothes, or the soles of his shoes, and so Kroll did not believe it was possible for him to have stuffed his pockets full of bricks, before climbing over a wall and then down onto the scaffolding to hang himself.

Calvi's autopsy found he had died at around 1:00 a.m., high tide on the Thames, and so with the water at about 30 feet (9 meters) high it was not possible to hang himself, as he would have been submerged in the water and the rope would have been slack. He had red marks around his neck and no river water in his lungs, so had been strangled and not drowned. It is believed he was possibly drugged, and strangled with a rope before being placed under the bridge. This could have been done at high tide from a small boat on the river.

Left to right: Silvano Vittor and Flavio Carboni were cleared of Calvi's murder in 2007.

Reopening the case

At first the report was dismissed, but in 2002 an Italian judge appointed forensic experts to study the evidence and declared Calvi had been murdered, which prompted City of London police to reopen their own case. There was a long list of aggrieved parties with a grudge against Calvi, including the Vatican, the Mafia, and a secretive branch of the Italian Masons, who all believed he had lost them significant amounts of money with Banco Ambrosiano's collapse.

The Vatican having any involvement in his death was explosive, but no solid evidence has ever been produced to implicate them. They were eventually granted immunity, although in 1984 agreed to pay $224 million to over 100 Banco Ambrosiano creditors as "recognition of a moral involvement."

For such a secret organization, Masons Propaganda Due having any role in Calvi's murder is inevitably shrouded in mystery, and is more rumor-driven than fact-based. It has been speculated that because their inner circle call themselves "Frati Neri" (Black Friars), Calvi was hung symbolically from the bridge of the same name.

It has long been suspected the Mafia were involved in Calvi's death, but again this has been difficult to prove. There have been claims that Mafia figures had ordered the hit on Calvi to keep him quiet about possible money laundering, and as revenge for losing such large amounts of their money.

It wasn't until 2005 that Italian authorities were able to issue criminal charges when five people went on trial in Rome: Sardinian businessman Flavio Carboni, his former girlfriend Manuela Kleinszig, Calvi's former bodyguard Silvano Vittor, and Mafia figures Pippo Calo and Ernesto Diotallevi. However, in June 2007, after nearly two years, all five were cleared of Calvi's murder, with the judge citing a lack of evidence. He also ruled that the banker's death was caused by murder, but by whom remains a mystery to this day.

THE
BOY IN
THE BOX

LOCATION: ................PHILADELPHIA, USA

VICTIM: ....UNKNOWN

DATE: ....FEBRUARY 25, 1957

The police were horrified at what they discovered when they went to investigate reports of a strange doll inside a cardboard box that had been discarded in woods on the edge of Philadelphia.

It was, in fact, the naked and battered body of a boy they estimated to be aged between four and six, who had been thrown out as if he was trash.

Who was this boy in the box, and why was he killed?

THE EVENTS

La Salle College student Frank Guthrum was walking through an area
of woods off the Susquehanna Road, in the northeast Philadelphia
neighborhood of Fox Chase, when he stumbled across a disturbing box.
He would claim he had followed a rabbit into the woods, or was checking on
rabbit traps, but it was suspected he had been trying to spy on the House of
the Good Shepherd, a home for what was described as wayward girls. There
in the woods he discovered a cardboard box with what appeared to be a large
doll protruding from it, and after some initial reluctance, something about it
troubled him enough to report it to the police.

Patrolman Elmer Palmer attended the scene, expecting to find nothing more
than a doll in an area well known to be where locals dumped waste. But
as soon as Palmer spotted the box, with a small head and shoulder visible
from the open side, he knew this was a real child. On closer inspection it
was ascertained this was a boy measuring 3 feet 3 inches tall (99 cm) and
weighing around 30 pounds (14 kg), who the
police believed was aged between four and six
years old.

The boy was naked, covered in bruises, clearly
malnourished, and had been wrapped in
a blanket before being placed in the box.
His body had been cleaned, his nails were
trimmed, and he had just been given a haircut,
probably at home rather than at a barber's, as
his chest was covered in fresh hair clippings.
There were surgical scars on his groin, ankle,
and underneath his chin, while the cause of
death was believed to be two blows to his
head. An experienced police captain was so
distressed by the state of the boy's body he
threw up at the scene.

Investigators believe the
mysterious boy in the box
had been given a haircut
just before he was killed.

The police were confident someone would come forward to say they knew the identity of the boy and this would be solved in a matter of days. There were 400,000 posters and leaflets produced with the boy's image, which could be found all over Philadelphia—on walls, in store windows, and added to every gas bill. The police even placed an appeal in a pediatric journal, highlighting the boy's multiple surgical scars, but frustratingly had no response to it.

The best lead was a man who contacted the police to say he had driven past these woods in Fox Chase and seen a woman and girl standing by a car at the side of the road. They were peering into an open trunk. The man said he offered to help them, but the woman refused and he kept driving. He did not see either of their faces in the brief exchange.

The police made the obvious enquiries, checking with every hospital, foster home, and orphanage in the area, but no children had been reported missing. As many as 270 policemen, consisting mainly of local academy recruits, would participate in a long search of the woods, and found a white handkerchief with the initial G on it, a child's scarf, and a child's blue corduroy cap.

The police had discovered a serial number inside the discarded box which revealed it had come from the J.C. Penney store in Upper Darby around 15 miles (25 km) away. It had been used to hold a baby's white bassinet, and 11 had been sold from that store. The police tracked down eight of the people who had purchased the bassinet, but the leads went nowhere.

Any early confidence in solving the case evaporated, and the police were left with no credible leads, just the sound of uneasy silence. As a detective working on the case told the fingerprint expert Billy Kelly, who had taken the boy's finger and foot prints on the day he was discovered: "This case is written in ice."

THE THEORIES

After all the leads went cold, two men, Bill Kelly and former medical examiner Remington Bristow, tried to crack the case. They both agreed the boy had been killed by his abusive parents, either biological or foster. They had a theory that because he was found clean and with a new haircut, he had possibly resisted them and been hit harder than usual, resulting in the bruises on his head. The parents or carers had panicked and hurriedly disposed of the body in the woods.

In 1960 Remington focused his investigations on a foster home near where the boy's body had been discarded, and found a bassinet similar to the one sold inside the J.C. Penney box. He invented a theory that the boy was the son of the stepdaughter of the couple who ran the foster home, and his body had been disposed of after an accident, but there was little evidence to support this and police dismissed it.

As recently as 2002, a woman known as "M" came forward to say her abusive mother had purchased the boy from his parents in 1954, and he had become the victim of abuse in their home. On the evening of his death, the boy had vomited up his dinner and been hit so hard he died from his injuries. M said her mother then cut the boy's hair to hide his identity, then enlisted her help to dump him in the woods. While they were preparing to lift him out of the trunk of their car, M recalls a male driver asking if they needed help, which fitted with evidence given in 1957. M's history of mental illness undermined her story, and police were unable to find any evidence a boy had lived in her house during the 1950s.

Kelly and Remington's other theory was as the boy had no vaccination scars, maybe he had been born outside the United States and arrived there as an immigrant. Again, though, this led nowhere.

Kelly found an article from 1956 about the arrival of Hungarians in the United States, and thought he spotted the boy in a photograph. He looked at over 11,000 passport photos and managed to track down the boy alive and well, living in North Carolina.

DEATH IN
BOLLYWOOD

LOCATION:.........................MUMBAI, INDIA

VICTIM:...............................JIAH KHAN

DATE:.............................JUNE 3, 2013

At the age of just 25, Jiah Khan appeared to have everything to live for: wealth, beauty, a famous boyfriend, and an exciting career as a Bollywood star—until she was found dead at an apartment in Mumbai.

The police and the authorities have long insisted the young star committed suicide, but her family refuse to accept this. What is the truth?

THE EVENTS

At a 2008 Bollywood awards ceremony, the host introduced the actress Jiah Khan as the Indian movie industry's newest "hot, beautiful, young, sexy star" before she performed a dance from her new movie *Ghajini*. Her role as Sunita would help *Ghajini* become Bollywood's highest grossing movie of that year, as Khan appeared to be living out her long-held dream of having a successful acting career.

Born in New York to Indian parents, Khan was educated and raised in London, UK, before moving to India to break in to the movie industry when she was 17. She made her debut in the critically acclaimed *Nishabd* before starring in *Ghajini* and the romantic comedy *Housefull* in 2010.

On the evening of June 3, 2013, Khan was at her family's apartment in the Mumbai beach suburb of Juhu, with simple plans to watch several episodes of *Game of Thrones*. She was also looking forward to seeing her youngest sister Kavita, who was arriving from London that night. "We bombarded each other with emojis," Kavita told the *Guardian* in 2017. "We couldn't wait to see each other."

Khan's mother Rabbiya left Jiah alone in the apartment at 9:00 p.m. to join friends for dinner. She spoke to her daughter on her cell just after 9:30 p.m., and recalls she appeared in a good mood—it was the last time the two would speak. At 11:20 p.m. Rabbiya returned home to find Jiah's body hanging from a ceiling fan in one of the apartment's bedrooms. Her mother has recalled how it must have just happened, as her body was still warm, but it was still too late to save her daughter.

At the time of her tragic death, Jiah Khan was emerging as a new young star in Bollywood.

How Jiah's body was found appeared to make this a straightforward case of suicide, which is what the local Mumbai police initially told the hordes of reporters who quickly gathered outside the apartment. The belief that Jiah had been driven to suicide after hiding an inner turmoil was only bolstered with the discovery of a six-page letter she had written before her death to her boyfriend Sooraj Pancholi:

"If you're reading this I might have already left or about to leave. I am broken inside. You may not have known this but you affected me deeply to a point where I lost myself in loving you. Yet you tortured me every day. These days I see no light. I wake up not wanting to wake up. There was a time I saw my life with you...But you shattered my dreams. I feel dead inside.

"I wish you had loved me like I loved you. I dreamed of our future. I dreamed of our success. I leave this place with nothing but broken dreams and empty promises. All I want now is to go to sleep and never wake up again. I am nothing. I had everything. I felt so alone even while with you. You made me feel alone and vulnerable. I am so much more than this."

THE THEORIES

In the eight years since her death, Jiah's family have strongly contested the theory she committed suicide. "We knew she couldn't have done it," her sister Kavita told the *Guardian* in 2017. "At first we simply trusted the police.

We thought they would uncover what had really happened, and who had done this to her."

The Mumbai police had concluded that Jiah's death was "suicidal in nature," but with the discovery of Jiah's letter they arrested Pancholi and charged him with abetting her suicide. However, within weeks the Bombay High Court ruled that Pancholi had not been responsible for her death.

Khan's former boyfriend Sooraj Pancholi has been arrested several times by police but has denied any involvement in her death.

Jiah's mother, Rabbiya, would not be deterred, and requested that India's Central Bureau of Investigation (CBI) take over the case. Her wish was granted, with the CBI questioning Pancholi and raiding his house in Mumbai during their investigations. He would be charged with abatement to suicide once again, but in August 2016 the CBI cleared him of any involvement and stated that Jiah's death was "suicide by hanging."

This would still not dissuade the Khan family that something more sinister had occurred that night. They have pointed to the fact Jiah had injuries on her face and arm, and there were unexplained spots of blood around her. The "suicide note" was dismissed as a simple farewell letter as she intended to go to London to return to her studies.

The white dupatta Jiah had allegedly used to hang herself was lost by police before it could be inspected, and the sweatsuit she had been wearing that night was never found by the police. The family have also wanted to know why no fingerprints were found in the room.

The Khan family have commissioned three independent forensic reports, including one from Englishman Jason Payne-James in 2016, who said he found evidence Jiah might have been killed before she was hung. He added there was a possibility it was a "staged hanging."

In January 2018 Pancholi was charged with abatement to suicide for a third time, but by the summer of 2021, more than three years later, there has been no further progress in the case, and a trial has yet to begin. Pancholi has always strenuously denied he had any involvement in Jiah's death.

4

MURDER MOST GRUESOME

This chapter is not for the
faint-hearted, as we look at some
of the most gruesome and bloody
murders in history, including
The St. Valentine Day's Massacre,
when six mobsters were mowed
down with machine guns in Chicago,
and the Wonderland murders, when
four members of an infamous drug
gang were battered to death in
their beds by a rival gang
wielding hammers.

THE
BUTCHER OF
PLAINFIELD

LOCATION: PLAINFIELD, WISCONSIN, USA

SUSPECT: .... ED GEIN

VICTIMS: 2

DATE: 1947-57

The inspiration for Alfred Hitchcock's iconic movie *Psycho*, Ed Gein grew up ruled by his puritanical and controlling mother, Augusta.

After her death he turned to murder and grave snatching to feed his warped fantasies—until police found his house decorated with a macabre collection of human heads, skulls, and skin-covered furniture.

What motivated the sickening acts of "The Butcher of Plainfield"?

THE EVENTS

In the sleepy hamlet of Plainfield, Wisconsin, Ed Gein was considered to be a simple but harmless character who tended to his farm and did small handyman jobs in the local area. This was until the evening of November 16, 1957, when police arrived at the remote farmhouse where he had lived on his own for over a decade since the death of his beloved mother, Augusta.

The police were searching the house following the disappearance of local hardware store owner Bernice Worden. Her son Deputy Sheriff Frank Worden had visited the store to find its cash register open and bloodstains on the floor. He knew Gein had been at the store the previous evening, when he had stated he would return the next morning to purchase some antifreeze, which was the last receipt his mother had written that morning.

Inside a barn on Gein's property was the body of 57-year-old Bernice, who had been shot with a .22-calibre rifle at the store, and was found hanging

A police officer examines Ed Gein's cluttered kitchen, where human skulls and body parts were found.

Gein is led away by police after his arrest in November 1957.

upside down from the rafters with ropes on her wrists. She had been decapitated and her torso sliced fully open; hunters would compare it to being "dressed out like a deer." Her head was found in a sack, and her heart was hanging in a plastic bag near to Gein's potbelly stove.

On searching the rest of the house, the police soon found a collection of keepsakes that included bowls made from human skulls, a belt made from female nipples, and a lampshade made from a human face. There was also a wastebasket, leggings, masks, a corset, and chair seat covers all made from human skin, a pair of lips on a window shade drawstring, and a collection of skulls, noses, female vulvas, and fingernails. The skull of Mary Hogan, a local tavern owner missing since 1954, was also found.

Gein confessed to the murders of Worden and Hogan, and told police he had acquired the rest of his collection by digging up bodies from local graveyards in up to 40 nighttime visits between 1947 and 1952. He would tan the body parts and/or skin, and then use them in household items and clothing.

Gein was charged with murder, but after being diagnosed with schizophrenia was declared unfit for trial and sent to a hospital for the criminally insane. Eleven years later, Gein's doctors said he was fit enough to participate in a trial, which started in November 1968. Gein's memory was unreliable, although he recalled being in Worden's store and may have accidentally shot her. He admitted killing Hogan, but was never tried for her murder. Gein was found guilty of murder, but in a second trial declared criminally insane and sentenced to spend the rest of his life in a mental hospital. He died there at the age of 77, in July 1984.

THE THEORIES

What had turned Gein into a cold-blooded killer who liked to decorate his house with such a grim array of body parts? It has long been theorized Gein's warped relationship with his mother was the biggest influence behind his crimes. His childhood was dominated by Augusta's strict and controlling behavior, and he simultaneously hated and loved her. He felt rejected, but also sought her love and admiration, which he found difficult to gain.

Born in 1906, Gein moved with his family in 1915 to the farm in Plainfield that would become their home for the next four decades. Gein's father was an alcoholic who drifted between jobs. Ed and his older brother Henry led a sheltered life, only allowed to leave the house to attend school. Whenever Ed showed any interest in making friends, he was punished by his mother.

A committed Lutheran, Augusta would preach to her boys about the evils of the world, particularly women, who were sinful creatures to be shunned. She would read them passages from the Bible, and plead with them to remain pure and not to give in to lust and carnal desires.

In 1940 Gein's father passed away, and four years later Henry died in a mysterious bush fire on the family's property. For a year, Ed and Augusta lived together, until she suffered a stroke and died in 1945. She had been a constant in his life, and as Harold Schechter said in his 1989 book *The Shocking True Story of the Original Psycho*, Gein had now "lost his only friend and one true love. And he was absolutely alone in the world."

Gein boarded up the rooms used by his mother, including her bedroom and living room, and left her belongings and clothes untouched. It was suggested Augusta's preaching and attitudes to sex had created a deranged and psychotic son who turned to murder and grave snatching. It was also reported that Gein created a woman's suit from the skin he procured from graveyards so he could fit inside it and pretend to be his mother.

DEATH
IN PERUGIA

LOCATION: .... PERUGIA, ITALY

SUSPECTS: 3

VICTIM: .... MEREDITH KERCHER

DATE: .... NOVEMBER 1, 2007

A British exchange student in the Italian city of Perugia was found dead on her bedroom floor, covered in seven cuts and 16 bruises.

During a bungled investigation, the finger of blame was initially pointed at her American housemate, Amanda Knox, but who did kill Meredith Kercher?

THE EVENTS

In the fall of 2007, 21-year-old Meredith Kercher set off for a new adventure as an exchange student at the University of Perugia, amid the beauty of Umbria. She had been studying at the University of Leeds, in the UK, but had fallen in love with Italy, and was looking forward to immersing herself in its culture and language.

"She fought so hard to get out there," her father John told the BBC. "There were quite a few setbacks, but she was determined to go and kept persisting, and eventually got what she wanted."

Kercher moved into a house on Via della Pergola, where she lived with two older women, Filomena Romanelli and Laura Mezzetti, and 20-year-old American student Amanda Knox, who was on exchange from the University of Washington. To begin with, Kercher and Knox both enjoyed getting to know their new home with each other, experiencing Perugia's vibrant social scene, and attending a music concert and a chocolate festival together.

"The two were like chalk and cheese, totally opposite in character," 24-year-old Giacomo Silenzi, who knew them both, has said. "Meredith was calm, sweet, and shy. Amanda was an extrovert and always showing off."

On the evening of November 1, which was a public holiday in Italy, Kercher had dinner with three other English women in the city before returning home at around 8:45 p.m. Meanwhile, on that same night, Knox was at the house of her new boyfriend Raffaele Sollecito, a fellow student at the university, and returned home the following morning on November 2.

Amanda Knox arrived in Italy to study at the University of Perugia in the fall of 2007.

There, she found the front door open and drops of blood on the bathroom floor, but Kercher's bedroom door was locked so she assumed she was still asleep. Knox would return later with Sollecito to discover a broken window in Romanelli's bedroom and still no answer from behind Kercher's door.

The police were summoned to the house and Kercher's door was forced open. Her body was discovered lying on the floor underneath a duvet, her throat cut. An autopsy found her body covered in seven cuts and 16 bruises on her face, which suggested her killer had clamped his hand down around her mouth. The report also suggested Kercher may have been sexually assaulted, as she had injuries around her groin. On November 6, Knox and Sollecito were arrested, along with 38-year-old Congolese barman Patrick Lumumba, and held on suspicion of conspiracy to commit murder and sexual assault.

THE THEORIES

The Perugia police said that Knox kept changing her story, and at one point she admitted she had covered her ears as Kercher screamed in her bedroom, which she would later retract. According to the *Guardian*, police claimed Kercher was murdered because she refused to take part in a violent sex game. Knox and Sollecito denied this, but were remanded in custody for a year.

A week after the arrest, the police stated Kercher's DNA had been found on a kitchen knife belonging to Sollecito. In November Lumumba was released without charge.

After his bloody fingerprints were found at the crime scene on Kercher's pillow, police named 20-year-old Ivory Coast national Rudy Guede as another suspect. He had fled to Germany two days after the murder, but was extradited back to Italy and charged.

Knox's boyfriend Raffaele Sollecito was found guilty of Kercher's murder before eventually being cleared.

In September 2008 Guede opted for a fast-track trial to be held separately to Knox and Sollecito. He told the court he had been at Kercher's house on the night she was murdered, but was not responsible for her death. Guede said he had arranged a date with Kercher and arrived at her house at 9:00 p.m. They had kissed, but when he left the bedroom to use the bathroom, he heard her scream, and saw a figure holding a knife, standing over her body.

Guede's account was not believed by the judge, with the most damning evidence being the discovery of his bloody fingerprints inside the house, and he was found guilty of murder and sentenced to 30 years' imprisonment, which in 2010 was reduced to 16 years.

In January 2009 Knox and Sollecito's trial got underway, with the prosecution arguing they had attacked Kercher with Guede in her bedroom, and helped the Ivorian sexually abuse her. They claimed Knox had delivered the fatal stab wound, and then made it look like the house had been burgled.

Knox protested her innocence and told the court, "I'm afraid of having the mask of a murderer forced onto my skin," but the judges found them both guilty. Knox was imprisoned for 26 years, and Sollecito 25 years.

The pair launched an appeal that began in November 2010, and over the course of a year, the judges heard how the DNA found at the crime scene could have been contaminated by a dirty glove, and Kercher's DNA was not on the murder weapon. In October 2011 Knox and Sollecito were acquitted; in March 2013 the acquittals were overturned because of the handling of the appeals process, and in January 2014 the guilty verdicts were reinstated.

In March 2015 this long, winding process finally came to an end when Italy's Supreme Court ruled Knox and Sollecito were innocent and completely exonerated. The court declared that there was no evidence the pair were at the crime scene, and none of their "biological traces" were in the room either.

THE
BLOODY
BENDER FAMILY

LOCATION: ....KANSAS, USA

SUSPECT: 4

VICTIMS: ....UP TO 20

DATE: 1870-73

When a group of local people searched the Bender family's property,
they were horrified to discover a blood-splattered basement and
up to 11 mutilated bodies buried in shallow graves in the yard.
The victims all had cut throats and had been hit over the head with
a hammer.

How did the Benders become a family of serial killers?

THE EVENTS

In October 1870, the Bender family arrived in the township of Osage in Labette County, in the northwest of Kansas. John Bender Senior ("Pa") and his son John Bender Junior settled here and claimed around 160 acres of land, before they were joined by John Senior's wife Elvira ("Ma") and their daughter Kate. The family erected a small home with just one room, which they divided with a curtain into two spaces. At the back were their living quarters, at the front a general store. Here the Benders would serve meals to hungry travelers, allowing some to spend the night. Kate would also offer them her psychic skills.

The house was near the Great Osage Trail, which was always busy with travelers headed West. It could be a dangerous place, with frequent attacks by Native Americans and bandits, or accidents caused by rocky roads and old wagons. It was soon noticed several people had gone missing when passing through Labette County, and wary travelers began to choose different routes. Between May 1871 and February 1872, the bodies of three men were found in this area, with their throats cut and skulls caved in. No arrests were made.

This wood engraving from 1873 shows the excavated grave sites of eight of the murderous family's victims.

In March 1873 a Dr. William York went missing near the trail. The doctor's two brothers, Ed York and Colonel Alexander M. York, went searching for him, and by March 28 had made their way to the Benders' house, where they enquired if they had seen him. The Benders said they recalled seeing Dr. York at their house in recent weeks, and suggested he might have experienced trouble with Native Americans. The family grew angry when asked about reports a young woman had been threatened with knives at their house.

Search party

The Osage community could no longer ignore the amount of mysterious deaths and disappearances occurring, and called for a community meeting. There were 75 people in attendance, including Colonel York and both John Bender Senior and Junior, and together they agreed to search every homestead in their township between Big Hill Creek and Drum Creek.

Three days after the meeting, neighbors began to notice the Benders' house seemed abandoned, their farm animals untamed and unfed. Volunteers gathered, along with Colonel York, to search the house, where they stumbled across a trap door in the floor. A basement was revealed, with a pungent smell in the air—and clotted blood on the walls. The group looked for bodies by smashing the stone floor with sledgehammers, and even lifted up the house and dug under its foundations. Finding Dr. York's body buried, face up in the yard, the group would soon unearth the bodies of seven more victims.

The grave of Dr. William Henry York, whose disappearance ultimately led to the discovery of the Benders' gruesome activities.

All had been killed in the same way: their throats slit and hit in the head with what was believed to be a hammer. There has never been a definitive number of bodies found in this search, but it is believed to be between 8 and 11. The Benders' total number of victims could be closer to 20.

THE THEORIES

Investigators soon formed a theory as to how the Benders had killed so many. A guest at their house would be given a place at their family table with their back to a curtain, from behind which one of the Bender men would appear and smash the victim in the head with a hammer before cutting the victim's throat. The Benders would dispose of the body through the trap door, before stripping and robbing the victim, then buried the body in a shallow grave. The motive was possibly robbery, as it was estimated their killing spree gained them thousands of dollars in cash.

A succession of men came forward to say they had almost become another one of the Benders' victims and were subjected to this routine. William Pickering said, when he refused to sit near the curtain he was threatened with a knife by Kate Bender and quickly left; a Mr. Wetzell also declined to sit in the "murder seat," causing Elvira Bender to abuse him, so he made his excuses and left; and a Catholic priest who was dining at the house felt uncomfortable when he saw one of the family hiding a large hammer, and so also got up and left.

Authorities followed the Benders' wagon tracks to the city of Thayer, just north of their house, where they boarded trains. It is believed John Senior and Elvira's destination was St. Louis, in Missouri, while Kate and John Junior made it south, to near the border between Texas and New Mexico.

A number of vigilante groups were formed to find the Benders, tempted by reward money. There were several unverified tales the Benders had been caught and killed, but the money was never claimed.

THE SAINT VALENTINE'S DAY MASSACRE

LOCATION:.........................CHICAGO, USA

VICTIMS:...7

DATE:.......................FEBRUARY 14, 1929

A horrible stench of blood and smoke hung in the air when police arrived at a garage on the North Side of Chicago to find six bodies on the floor and an injured man taking his final gasps of breath.

Moments earlier, this had been the site of one of the most famous crimes in U.S. history, when seven men had been mowed down in what would become known as the St. Valentine's Day Massacre.

Who was responsible for this horrific hail of bullets?

THE EVENTS

At 10:30 a.m. on a cold Chicago morning, a black Cadillac stopped outside the S.M.C. Cartage Company on 2122 North Clark Street. Four men exited the car—two wearing smart suits, two in police uniform—and walked into the nondescript garage through the front door.

The garage was rented by local crime boss George "Bugs" Moran, the head of the North Side Gang who had come to control the area's supply of illegal alcohol during Prohibition, as well as running several casinos and brothels. The dimly lit garage was used by Moran and his associates to store their alcohol and guns, and to park and repair their fleet of vehicles.

On that day there were seven men inside the garage: John May, a mechanic for the gang; convicted armed robber and Moran's second in command, Albert Kachellek; two of the gang's enforcers, Peter and Frank Gusenberg; one of the gang's business managers, Adam Heyer; and a local optician, Reinhardt Schwimmer, who enjoyed consorting with them.

Mass execution

When the four men come through the front door, these seven men didn't reach for their guns, but, probably due to the presence of two "police officers," complied with their order to line up in a row against the garage's back wall. Without warning, the four men produced two submachine guns and two shotguns, and opened fire with a hail of around 90 bullets that saw all seven men fall to the concrete floor in a pool of their collective blood.

The four shooters strolled calmly from the building and got back into their Cadillac, with eyewitnesses recalling it appeared as though the two "police officers" were leading the other two men out at gunpoint, a calculated ruse to suggest the criminals had been arrested.

When police arrived at the scene they found seven men on the floor, six of them already dead, and a seventh, Frank Gusenberg, hanging on to life, but he would later die in hospital.

THE THEORIES

The most plausible theory has long been the massacre represented the climax of Chicago's bloody turf war between Moran's North Side Gang and the South Side Gang, led by the infamous Al Capone. It has been speculated Capone ordered the hit against Moran and his associates to seize control of the city's growing bootleg trade.

Moran, who liked to mock his rival as "The Beast," had been getting increasingly confident in their escalating feud, grabbing some of Capone's illegal drinking dens and muscling in to his gambling businesses at local dog tracks. Capone also had reason to believe Moran's gang was responsible for hijacking a truck of illegal whiskey he had brought in from Canada, and the murders of two of his close associates, Pasqualino "Patsy" Lolordo and Antonio "The Scourge" Lombardo.

It is likely Moran was intended to be another one of the victims of the massacre, but on his way to the garage he, along with gang member Ted Newberry, noticed a police car and quickly hid inside a nearby café.

Crowds watch on as police stretcher out the bodies from the garage in which they were brutally gunned down.

Capone seemed to have a watertight alibi for the crime, as when it took place he was nearly 1,400 miles (2,300 km) away in Dade County, Florida, where he was speaking to investigators about the death of his former mentor Frankie Yale. He had an obvious motive to take down Moran, but the police needed more. They would charge Capone's associates John Scalise and Jack McGurn with being involved in the massacre, but in May 1929 Capone had Scalise killed, along with Albert Anselmi and Joseph "Hop Toad" Giunta. The charge against McGurn was later dropped through lack of evidence.

In December 1929 a renowned bank robber with ties to Capone, called Fred "Killer" Burke, killed a policeman in St. Joseph, Michigan, and when his house was searched they discovered a huge cache of guns, including two machine guns, which ballistic tests proved had been used in both the St. Valentine's Day Massacre and the murder of Yale. Strangely, the police never asked Burke if Capone had recruited him for the massacre. Instead Burke went on the run for over a year, but when he was finally captured the police were more interested in charging him with the murder of their colleague. He was sentenced to life in prison, but died in 1940 from a heart attack, and never provided any answers why he had the guns.

In January 1935 another bank robber, called Byron Bolton, who was in custody for another crime, confessed to being involved in the massacre in a deal to reduce his prison sentence. He said Capone had ordered the hit against Moran, and he was there as the lookout for the killers, who were Burke and four other men. One of the killers he named proved to have an alibi, but again the investigation went nowhere, and authorities took no action against Bolton.

There were other rumors Moran had ordered the hit against his own gang, who were possibly betraying him, or that others, including Egan's Rats or the Purple Gang from Detroit, were responsible, but no one has ever been convicted.

THE LINDBERGH KIDNAPPING

LOCATION:...................NEW JERSEY, USA

SUSPECT:................RICHARD HAUPTMANN

VICTIM:....CHARLES LINDBERGH, JUNIOR

DATE:...........................MARCH 1, 1932

When a delivery truck driver pulled to the side of a New Jersey road and ventured into the woods to relieve himself, he stumbled across the decomposed body of a child.

He had found Charles Lindbergh, Junior, the son of the famous aviator Charles Lindbergh, who had been reported missing for two months.

Who had stolen the child from his bed and murdered him?

THE EVENTS

Charles Lindbergh was a renowned aviator, inventor, and activist, most famous for being the first person to fly solo nonstop across the Atlantic between New York and Paris in 1927.

On the evening of March 1, 1932, Lindbergh and his wife Anne were enjoying a quiet time at their home near Hopewell, New Jersey. Their 20-month-old son Charles had been suffering with a cold in recent days, and at around 7:30 p.m. his nanny Betty Gow had rubbed some medication on his chest before she returned to check on him at 10:00 p.m.—to find his crib empty. The nanny immediately alerted the baby's father, who stormed upstairs to the bedroom. "I immediately noticed a lifted window," Lindbergh recalled. "A strange-looking envelope lay on the sill. I looked at the crib. It was empty. I ran downstairs, grabbed my rifle, and went out into the night."

Accompanied by his butler Olly Whateley, Lindbergh found marks in the ground underneath his son's bedroom window and parts of a homemade wooden ladder, and later muddy footprints on the carpet next to the crib.

The strange-looking envelope on the bedroom window sill contained a semiliterate ransom note, which demanded $50,000 for the return of the baby, and the kidnapper said they would be back in touch within two to four days.

The police launched an investigation, but Lindbergh was not content to rely solely on them and reached out to several intermediaries, including organized-crime figures, most notably Al Capone, to see if they knew who was behind his son's kidnapping.

Five days after the baby's disappearance, another note from the kidnappers arrived at Lindbergh's

Charles Lindbergh was only 20 months old when he was kidnapped from his bedroom.

Charles Lindbergh attended the trial of Richard Hauptmann (pictured), who would be found guilty of murdering his son.

home informing him they had raised the ransom to $70,000. There soon followed another note informing Lindbergh he should only deal with a man named John Condon as an intermediary. Condon was a 72-year-old retired teacher from the Bronx who had written a letter to the *Bronx Home News* offering his help, and then been contacted by the kidnappers. Lindbergh gave his approval to Condon acting on his behalf.

A series of meetings was organized through classified ads where Condon would meet a man at Woodlawn Cemetery in the Bronx. But the man stayed in the shadows, never revealing his face, and became known as "Cemetery John." Only after the kidnapper had proved he had the baby, by sending the sleeping suit the baby was wearing when taken, would Lindbergh agree to pay the ransom.

On the night of April 2, Condon, with Lindbergh waiting nearby in a car, met "Cemetery John" at St. Raymond's Cemetery in the Bronx. He managed to negotiate the ransom down to the original $50,000, and handed over a distinctive wooden box with the ransom made up of gold certificates and cash, with the serial numbers recorded to track use. In return, the kidnapper informed Condon that the baby would be found on a boat called *Nelly* between Horseneck Beach and Gay Head, near the Elizabeth Islands north of Martha's Vineyard in Massachusetts, but when Lindbergh rushed to this location he found nothing.

On May 12, the decomposed body of Charles Lindbergh, Junior, was found in woods next to a road in Mount Rose less than 5 miles (8 km) from his house. An autopsy found he had been killed with a single blow to the head.

THE THEORIES

Police had laid their trap by giving the kidnapper a box of recorded dollar bills and gold certificates, and over the following two and half years tracked them being used in various cities, including New York, Chicago, and Minneapolis. Throughout 1934 the police noticed use of the bills was becoming concentrated in the Bronx neighborhood of Yorkville, before a tip-off from a gas station manager led them to arrest Richard Hauptmann.

A German immigrant carpenter, Hauptmann was found to be in possession of over $14,000 of the ransom money when police searched his house. He claimed his friend and former business partner Isidor Fisch had left a shoebox with him when he returned to Germany, where Fisch died in March 1934, and only learned later it contained money, which he believed he was entitled to, as Fisch was in his debt.

Further searches of Hauptmann's home also uncovered John Condon's telephone number, a sketch of a ladder similar to the one used to kidnap the Lindbergh baby, and, most damning of all, a piece of wood experts believed was used to construct the ladder found on the night of the kidnapping.

In January 1935 Hauptmann stood trial in the small town of Flemington, New Jersey, which drew a huge amount of public interest and was billed as the "Trial of the Century" by the newspapers. The prosecution's best evidence was the discovery of those items at Hauptmann's house, as well as Lindbergh's own testimony that the accused had the same voice as the shadowy figure he met at the graveyard. After a month the jury returned their verdict that Hauptmann was guilty of murder in the first degree. He was sentenced to death.

Hauptmann always maintained his innocence, and even when given the chance to reduce his sentence to life imprisonment refused to issue a confession before he was electrocuted at 8:44 p.m. on April 3, 1936.

CASE CLOSED

THE
HELLO KITTY

MURDER

LOCATION: ....HONG KONG

SUSPECTS: 3

VICTIM: ....FAN MAN-YEE

DATE: ....APRIL 15, 1999

A scene of unimaginable depravity greeted the Hong Kong police when they broke down the door of an apartment in the city's Tsim Sha Tsui district.

Here they discovered human teeth on the floor, human organs in the fridge, and, on closer inspection, a human skull sewn into the head of a Hello Kitty mermaid plush toy.

Over the course of a month, a young woman had been subjected to a brutal campaign of torture, before being killed and dismembered.

How had Fan Man-yee's life come to end in this sordid apartment?

THE EVENTS

In May 1999 a distressed 14-year-old girl walked into a Hong Kong police station with the unusual complaint that the ghost of a woman who had been tortured to death was haunting her. The teenager explained that each night this ghost drenched in blood visited her and she was desperate for it to stop.

At first the police dismissed this as a case of the girl either being delusional or simply experiencing nightmares—until she confessed she had played a role in the recent torture and death of the woman. The girl led the police to a third-floor apartment on Granville Road, in the city's Tsim Sha Tsui district, where they discovered a woman had been murdered and her skull sewn into the head of a Hello Kitty mermaid toy.

The skull belonged to missing 23-year-old nightclub hostess and prostitute Fan Man-yee, who had spent the final month of her life kept hostage in this derelict apartment.

A month earlier, Man-yee had been brought to the apartment as a punishment for stealing money from three men, known to be members of the organized crime group the Triads: 34-year-old Chan Man-lok, 27-year-old Leung Shing-cho, and 20-year-old Leung Wai-lun. Man-yee had apparently taken Man-lok's wallet containing HK$4,000 but quickly

The skull of Fan Man-Yee was found sewn inside the head of a Hello Kitty plush toy.

returned it, only to be told she would have to pay back the greater amount of HK$10,000 as both interest and an apology. She was unable to find this much money, and so the men found her on the street, bundled her into a car, and took her to the unfurnished apartment.

The group's initial plan had been to keep her captive and prostitute her out to other men to pay off her debt to them; however, this was quickly changed to what would become a month-long campaign of torture. Man-yee was tied up, raped, and beaten every day with bats, weapons, and pieces of furniture. The three men would also drip candle wax on her, and burn the bottom of her feet to ensure she was unable to escape. She was simultaneously starved and force-fed her own feces and urine, and toward the end of her captivity she was hung upside down from the ceiling and used as a human punch bag.

The men would play video games, eat meals, and take crystal meth in the presence of Man-yee's battered and increasingly diseased body. They would often be joined by the girl who had walked into the police station, known in court papers by the alias Ah Fong. She was described as Man-lok's girlfriend, and probably worked for him as a prostitute. Ah Fong admitted that she had sometimes taken part in Man-yee's torture, including an occasion when she helped Man-lok kick the victim in the head over 50 times. "I had a feeling it was for fun," she said.

BACKGROUND

Little is known about Fan Man-yee's life before it met such a gruesome end in that Hong Kong apartment. It is believed she was abandoned by her family as a young child and raised in a series of orphanages.

As a teenager she was quickly lured into Hong Kong's underworld, where she became both a prostitute and a drug addict. In 1997, aged 21, she met Chan-Man-lok, a pimp and drug dealer, at a nightclub, and he soon got her working for him to pay for her addiction.

On the evening of April 15, the three men and the girl went out for dinner and locked Man-yee in the bathroom. On their return, she was found dead. The group reasoned it would be easier to dispose of her body in parts rather than transport it as one, and so proceeded to dismember her in the bathroom. The men then placed various body parts in pots of boiling water on their stove to remove the flesh from her bones and conceal the smell of rotting flesh, before disposing of them in the garbage. There were also reports that the men cooked their meals of noodles in pots alongside these boiling body parts.

There was a debate about what to do with Man-yee's skull, and for reasons that have never been explained, they decided to stuff it inside the head of a Hello Kitty mermaid plush toy and sew it up.

Over the course of a six-week trial, in exchange for immunity the 14-year-old girl testified against the three men with details of their campaign of depravity. The defendants argued Man-yee had died of a drug overdose, which she had willfully taken herself, but this was dismissed by the jury. However, they were convicted of the lesser charge of manslaughter, as it could not be proven they intended to kill her. They were each sentenced to 20 years without parole.

"Never in Hong Kong in recent years has a court heard of such cruelty, depravity, callousness, brutality, violence, and viciousness," said Hong Kong Justice Peter Nguyen. "The public is entitled to protection from people such as you."

As the girl had said she had seen Man-yee's ghost, the apartment on Granville Road became a focus of fascination for people interested in the paranormal, many of whom went there to meet the ghost themselves, until the building was demolished in 2012.

THE
WONDERLAND
MURDERS

LOCATION:................LOS ANGELES, USA

VICTIMS: 4

DATE:..........................JULY 1, 1981

A removal man working on Wonderland Avenue in Los Angeles alerted police after he heard persistent groans coming from a house.

Inside, the police discovered four bodies and a woman barely still alive, surrounded by blood-splattered walls, who had been the victims of a frenzied attack.

Who was responsible for the murders of the Wonderland Gang?

THE EVENTS

During the late 1970s and early 1980s, a two-bedroom townhouse at 8763 Wonderland Avenue, in the Laurel Canyon neighborhood of Los Angeles, became known as the base for a renowned group of drug dealers. Taking their name from the avenue, the Wonderland Gang were a brutal collection of criminals who ruled through violence and fear at the heart of the city's lucrative cocaine trade.

They were led by Ron Launius, who had been dishonorably discharged from the U.S. Army for smuggling heroin back from Vietnam, and later served three years in federal prison for running drugs across the Mexican border. "One of the coldest people I ever met," was how a police officer described him. Launius presided over a gang of dangerous misfits that included his second-in-command Billy DeVerell, David Lind, Tracy McCourt, and Joy Miller.

The townhouse at 8763 Wonderland Avenue in Laurel Canyon, where the murders took place in July 1981.

On the night of June 30, 1981, three of the gang—Launius, DeVerell, and Miller—were at the house on Wonderland Avenue, accompanied by Launius's wife Susan and Lind's girlfriend Barbara Richardson. At around 3:00 a.m. a group of three or four men entered the house holding lead pipes and hammers—and viciously beat to death four of the gang.

Richardson was bludgeoned to death in the living room of the house, next to a couch she had been sleeping on; DeVerell and Miller were murdered together in the same bedroom, where a hammer was found; while Launius was killed as he lay on his bed in another room. Next to Launius was his wife Susan, who survived but was left with severe brain damage and would have to have part of her skull removed, as well as losing some of a finger. She could recall nothing about that night.

Porn star and addict John Holmes leaves Superior Court, acquitted of all charges.

Neighbors remember hearing someone scream, "Oh God, don't kill me!" during the attack, but, wearied by the constant noise and commotion that came from the house, dismissed it as just another raucous party. It wasn't until later that day, at around 4:00 p.m., that a removal man heard Susan Launius's groans and finally alerted the police. Walking around the ransacked house, the police were visibly shocked at how much blood was on the walls.

THE THEORIES

On June 29, two days before the attack, four members of the Wonderland Gang—Launius, DeVerell, Lind, and McCourt—had staged an armed robbery at the Los Angeles house of rival drug dealer Eddie Nash. Brandishing fake police badges, the gang gained entry to the house before shooting one of Nash's bodyguards, Gregory Diles. They held Nash at gunpoint, stealing jewelry, drugs, guns, and large amounts of cash.

Nash immediately suspected that the famous porn star John Holmes, who made over 500 movies, had helped the Wonderland Gang in the attack. By this time, Holmes's movie career had suffered through his addiction to cocaine, and he fed his habit with supplies from both Nash and the Wonderland Gang.

It is alleged, to pay off a debt Holmes helped the Wonderland Gang rob from Nash by drawing them a map to show where they would find his drugs and cash. On June 29, Holmes had spent up to six hours at Nash's house, and purposefully left open a side door to facilitate the attack. It is believed Nash then co-opted Holmes to take part with him in a revenge attack on the Wonderland Gang on July 1, and police would later find his palm print above the headboard on the bed where Launius's body was found.

In March 1982 Holmes was charged with the four murders at the Wonderland house, but during a three-week trial his lawyers successfully argued he was a victim himself, forced to attend the attack by Nash, who had threatened his family. The palm print was explained by the fact Holmes was a regular guest at the house. In June that same year, Holmes was acquitted of all the charges.

Eddie Nash is taken from
his home by police and
federal agents after a
raid on the house.

BACKGROUND

One of Los Angeles' most infamous drug dealers, Eddie Nash was born Adel
Gharib Nasrallah in British Palestine in 1929. He was the youngest son to a
family who owned up to 48 hotels across the region, but after the creation of
Israel he emigrated to the United States.

Nash claimed he had arrived with less than $10 in his pocket before attempting
to become an actor. After a couple of small roles he instead opened a hot dog
stand called Beef's Chuck on Hollywood Boulevard.

He would later expand into nightclubs and restaurants, and amass a property
empire worth an estimated $30 million, which also gave him a collection of
venues, including The Starwood and The Kit Kat Club, to deal drugs
to customers.

Nash died at the age of 85 in August 2014.

In March 1988 Holmes would die aged 43 from infections caused by contracting the AIDS virus, and though police were unsuccessful in getting him to provide a deathbed confession, a month later his first wife Sharon Holmes said he had told her about his role in the attack. On the day of the murders, Holmes arrived at the house he shared with Sharon in clothes covered in blood, and confessed he had just helped three men gain entry to the Wonderland house before watching them bludgeon to death the four victims. He never revealed who committed the murders.

Prime suspect

Eddie Nash became the prime suspect in the case, with police having found items stolen from the Wonderland house at his house. Finally, in 1990, he was charged with having planned the murders, but at the end of the trial, a hung jury vote of 11–1 in favor of conviction allowed him to walk free. It was suspected Nash had bribed the lone juror holding out.

Both local and federal authorities refused to give up on Nash, and in 2000, after a four-year investigation, arrested him again on multiple charges. The following year, Nash accepted a plea bargain in which he admitted to money laundering and jury tampering, having paid $50,000 to a woman juror in his earlier trial. He denied being involved in the Wonderland murders, but admitted to sending associates to the house to retrieve stolen property. Nash was fined $250,000 and received a four-and-a-half-year prison sentence, but with time already served, spent only a year in a federal facility.

CASE OPEN

FURTHER READING

Amirante, Sam L.; Broderick, Danny. *John Wayne Gacy: Defending a Monster*.
Skyhorse Publishing, 2011

Bennett, John; Gardner, Graham. *The Cromwell Street Murders:
The Detective's Story*. The History Press, 2011

Burn, Gordon. *Happy Like Murderers: The True Story of Fred and
Rosemary West*. Faber & Faber, 2019

Carlin, John. *Chase Your Shadow: The Trials of Oscar Pistorius*.
Atlantic Books, 2015

Clarkson, Wensley. *Evil Beyond Belief: The True Story of Harold Shipman,
Britain's Most Prolific Serial Killer*. John Blake, 2019

Eatwell, Piu. *Black Dahlia, Red Rose*. Coronet, 2018

Follain, John. *Death in Perugia: The Definitive Account of the Meredith Kercher
Case from her Murder to the Acquittal of Raffaele Sollecito and Amanda Knox*.
Hodder and Stoughton, 2011

Hainsworth, Jonathan; Ward-Agius, Christine. *The Escape of Jack the Ripper:
The Truth about the Cover-up and his Flight from Justice*.
Regnery History, 2021

Helmer, William J., Bilek; Arthur J. *The St. Valentine's Day Massacre:
The Untold Story of the Gangland Bloodbath that Brought Down Al Capone*.
Cumberland House Publishing, 2006

Kercher, John. *Meredith: Our Daughter's Murder and the Heartbreaking Quest
for the Truth*. Hodder and Stoughton, 2012

Lange, Tom; Souza, Rob. *Malice in Wonderland: The Inside Story of the
Police Investigation of the Laurel Canyon Murders*. LVM books, 2018

McNab, Duncan. *The Snapshot Killer: The Shocking True Story of Predator and Serial Killer Christopher Wilder—from Sydney's Beaches to America's Most Wanted*. Hachette Australia, 2021

Monier, Stephen; Ahlgren, Gregory; Caso, Adolph. *Crime of the Century: The Lindbergh Kidnapping Hoax*. Branden Books, 2009

O'Sullivan, Shane. *Who Killed Bobby? The Unsolved Murder of Robert F. Kennedy*. Union Square Press, 2008

Orth, Maureen. *Vulgar Favours; The Hunt for Andrew Cunanan, the Man who Killed Gianni Versace*. BBC books, 2017

Patterson, James. *The Last Days of John Lennon*. Arrow, 2001

Rubenhold, Haille. *The Five: The Untold Lives of the Women Killed by Jack the Ripper*. Black Swan, 2020

Schechter, Harold. *Hell's Princess: The Mystery of Belle Gunness, Butcher of Men*. Little A, 2018

Sullivan, Terry. *Killer Clown: The John Wayne Gacy Murders*. Pinnacle Books, 2013

Thomas, Steve. *JonBenét: Inside the Ramsey Murder Investigation*. St. Martin's Press, 2000

Thompson, Laura. *A Different Class of Murder: The Story of Lord Lucan*. Apollo, 2018

Toobin, Jeffery. *The People vs. O.J. Simpson: The Run of His Life*. Arrow, 2016

INDEX

CREDITS

The publisher would like to thank the following for the permission to reproduce copyright material:

Alamy: 30 REUTERS; 33 World History Archive; 41 Leonid Serebrennikov; 50 PA Images; 65 IanDagnall Computing; 66 PictureLux / The Hollywood Archive; 71 AF archive; 113 Trinity Mirror / Mirrorpix; 115 Nick Scott Archive; 165 & 166 Granger Historical Picture Archive; 177 Carolyn Jenkins

Getty: 7 Popperfoto; 11 Stefano Bianchetti; 12 Hulton Archive / Stringer; 17 Bettmann; 25 Getty Images / Handout; 35 Donaldson Collection; 36 Bettmann; 40 Laski Diffusion; 49L&R Universal History Archive; 57 Archive Photos / Stringer; 59 William Nation; 60 SAM MIRCOVICH / Stringer; 63 Michael Ochs Archives / Stringer; 70 Donaldson Collection; 72 Bettmann; 76 Andrew Shawaf; 79 Bettmann; 82 CHRIS BERNACCHI; 83 FBI / Handout; 87 Gallo Images; 89 BEN STANSALL / Stringer; 94 ROMEO GACAD / Stringer; 97 Alexander Hassenstein ; 99 Popperfoto; 100 Hulton Archive / Stringer; 103 STR / Stringer; 104 L&R CRIS BOURONCLE; 109 The Sydney Morning Herald; 114 Colin Davey; 116 Cate Gillon; 119 Axel Koester; 129 & 130 Bettmann; 132 New York Daily News Archive; 135 Terry Fincher / Stringer; 136 Express / Stringer; 138 Ian Tyas / Stringer; 143 Mondadori Portfolio; 144 ANDREAS SOLARO / Stringer; 151 & 152 Hindustan Times; 157 Bettmann; 158 Star Tribune via Getty Images; 161 & 162 Oli Scarff; 170 Chicago History Museum; 173 Mondadori Portfolio; 174 Hulton Archive / Stringer; 181 Kevin P. Casey; 182 Bettmann; 184 Boris Yaro

iStock: 14 duncan1890

Rex: 78 Shutterstock; 121 Sipa/Shutterstock

Shutterstock: 22 RAYphotographer; 39 John Williams RUS; 42 Vetertravel; 45 Marco Paulo Bahia Diniz; 69 MarinaMonroe; 75 Jonathan Weiss; 81 Tverdokhlib; 90 Trevor Christopher; 93 fifg; 125 Kemeo; 126 Photo Win1; 131 FrimuFilms; 141 balounm; 147 Rudenko Alla

While every effort has been made to credit photographers, The Bright Press would like to apologize should there have been any omissions or errors, and would be pleased to make the appropriate correction for future editions of the book.